Rev. Barbara

Keep walking th[...]
delivering the message and healing.
May the divinity in all things rise up
to meet you.

Namasté,
Balen A. Dur MD
7 November 2015

Heaven Abounds in You
The Journey to Joy

Balin A. Durr, M.D.

BALBOA.
PRESS
A DIVISION OF HAY HOUSE

Balboa Press books may be ordered through booksellers or by contacting:
Balboa Press
A Division of Hay House
1663 Liberty Drive
Bloomington, IN 47403
www.balboapress.com
1 (877) 407-4847

Because of the dynamic nature of the Internet, any web addresses or
links contained in this book may have changed since publication and
may no longer be valid. The views expressed in this work are solely those
of the author and do not necessarily reflect the views of the publisher,
and the publisher hereby disclaims any responsibility for them.

The author of this book does not dispense medical advice or prescribe the use
of any technique as a form of treatment for physical, emotional, or medical
problems without the advice of a physician, either directly or indirectly. The
intent of the author is only to offer information of a general nature to help you
in your quest for emotional and spiritual well-being. In the event you use any
of the information in this book for yourself, which is your constitutional right,
the author and the publisher assume no responsibility for your actions.

Printed in the United States of America.

ISBN: 978-1-4525-9017-2 (sc)
ISBN: 978-1-4525-9019-6 (hc)
ISBN: 978-1-4525-9018-9 (e)

Library of Congress Control Number: 2014900123

Balboa Press rev. date: 3/18/2014

"To me, art is a holy land where initiates seek to reveal the spirituality of matter. As such, art can be counted as one of the supreme sources of the triumph of the spirit."[1]

~ *James Washington Jr., Seattle Artist*

Dedication

To my children,
Hilary
(a.k.a. Madame Secretary)
and
Jaron
(a.k.a. the Little World Leader)
You are my love and light,
my heart in flight.
No Souls matter to me more than You.
You have my deep gratitude for agreeing
to take this journey with me.
I love you big much!

Contents

Journey's End...Until We Begin Again

Foreword

The God of my childhood, of which Dr. Balin A. Durr speaks, has been illuminated in her writings in a very poetic way. God, a Spirit, a Presence....poetry in motion is how God, the one we esteem as our Creator, is articulated throughout the pages of this eloquent writing. Dr. Durr writes of a God who is fluid and present and even unexpected; a Divine who cannot be marginalized by our construct of Him...Her.

After a worship experience at a church I visited recently, I dedicated time to take a walk down a quiet country road to meditate, to talk to God. I wanted to try and hear God's voice in the midst of the nature scenes that were created by the Divine. As I walked, I thought about many of the chapters that I had read in *Heaven Abounds in You*, and after much reflection, I realized I was making myself available to experience what had been there all along—God's presence. As Dr. Durr reminds us, we are created as an expression of Himself to be like Him. As she points out, there is no place where He is not and nowhere He has not been. So it is no wonder that I felt the presence of God in that worship experience that was unlike my own tradition, as well as in the space called nature that enveloped me as I walked in and through it.

No matter your theology, or even if you espouse none at all, Dr. Durr's writings will inspire you to "take a closer walk" with God, the Divine, your Center. Her writings will cause you to remove mortal limitations on how we construct our image of God and spur us to move ever so closer to the One who is our Source. After reading her work, I found her encouraging words nudged me to embrace all that life has to offer, even storms and loss because in all of life's experiences there is the God consciousness expressing itself in the form of love, hope....healing.

Still yourself and listen to God in these writing. Settle yourself and experience God in her words. Liberate yourself by knowing that God is, and where God is, peace abounds....Heaven abounds.

Rev. Valerie Toney Parker, MDiv., MBA

Acknowledgments

My parents, especially my mother, Mehlanie S. Spears, a powerful feminine presence who is dynamic, loving, creative, independent, courageous, and fierce! Some say I fell right underneath the tree.

Number One – You gave me air to soar, lifting me to joy!

Anthony Williams and Dr. General Hood – You are wise old Souls. I have learned much from the Masters.

Kerry – You brought me to the light with fun and laughter! Thank you for your friendship, love, and support.

David Jones and Selena Maynie – My friends, you were the first to ask, "When is your book coming out?" and you continued to do so until I had an answer. Thank you for that and the many other expressions of your friendship.

Dr. Faye Gary – One of my favorite people in the world! You loved, nurtured, and got me through residency. You are my ferry boat! I love you dearly.

Dr. Regnal "Pops" Jones – Thank you for your guidance, love, support, and being my "Pops." You are a true renaissance man.

C. "Dick" Benham, my mentor and friend. You taught me "Everything is in Divine order" and so much more. You knew who I'd become.

Leondo Phifer – Thank you for your enthusiasm, good heartedness, and tutelage in electricity and strategy.

Roy Woods – It is a blessing that you saw yourself in me then guided me around the obstacles. Thank you for your friendship.

Ian Dubé – Thank you for being my friend and coach. You have great vision and got me moving quickly!

Dr. Nathaniel E. Morgan, Jerome Cowthran, Kelly Williams, John Smith, William Hawkins, and Lisa Mencke – Thank you for your encouragement, guidance, and friendship.

Aunt Martha's Youth Service Center family: Jerry Lowell, Courtney Albert, Sonia Perez, Jan Sams, Dr. Jennifer Byrd, Joyce Wallace-Butler, Ana Gomez, Dr. Katrina Foster, Leann Lear, Judy Wissel, and Nicole Salvato – Thank you for the love, enthusiastic support, and yes, patience. You are awesome!

Kari Buishas, Dr. Kelley McKeever, Brenda Jepperson Vervlied – Thank you for your feedback and enthusiastic support.

Alison Boggs – Thank you for your editorial work especially in such a compressed period of time. I appreciate you greatly!

Dan Brown – To the rescue with your awesome graphic design work in record time! I can't say thank you enough.

To those who brought the storms, you taught me and strengthened me, and now I am so much more.

Thank you to the children, families, and adults who entrusted me with their healing. It has been my privilege to do so.

Ancestors – I stand upon your shoulders and endeavor to uphold your legacy.

Introduction

Welcome Home! Welcome to Your Self! This is a journey that leads you deep within. It is a thought-provoking exploration of who You are, your reason for Being here, and the Oneness of everything as an expression of the Divine Universal Source. It is no accident that you are reading this text at this time. Everything is in Divine order. This is an eclectic look at that journey in format and content. It is to and fro just as our journey is, just as Life is. There may be some surprises! This is not a sterile, sanitized version of spirituality. It is interlaced with Life as it is lived by human beings. It is expressed as our connection with each other and our connection with the Divine. It explores the heights and the depths of that journey as we attempt to remember that there is only One.

It is exciting that science is catching up and able to substantiate what some have known spiritually for millennia! All of this is old wisdom—only the presentation changes. How wisdom is presented makes all of the difference in the world. It's like seeing the spectrum of light reflected through a prism. Every rotation of the prism allows you to see a different color. It is my hope that you experience a spark of awakening or deepening of your knowing. We all awaken. It's just a matter of when.

My personal and professional journey as a child and adolescent psychiatrist is reflected in these pages. Ultimately, I am a healer, both for others and myself. I found that repeated exposure to medical information was necessary during my many years of psychiatric training. The Divine often presented the wisdom in this text to me in different contexts then revealed something new. So know that the capitalization of certain words and anything that appears repetitive is intentional. This wisdom is layered in order to facilitate your remembrance.

I refer to God or the Divine Universal Source by many names because there are many spokes to the center of the wheel. I refer to this Divine entity as "He" because this is the reference that was used as I grew up, but this is not meant to be limiting. My use of the term "It" at times is because He is Everything. It is not meant to be disrespectful. It is meant to be all encompassing as He Is. What I call Him seems less important than *knowing* who it is that I am speaking of or calling upon. As Shakespeare said, "that which we call a rose by any other name would smell as sweet."[2] For me, spirituality is about *being* connected to Him all of the time and living Life from that connection. There are many paths to the One.

Some of the quotes in this book are from family, friends, and the community. They are average, everyday "folk." Some might call them ordinary, but they are extraordinary in their wisdom and their ability to convey it in a way that most people will understand. Their wisdom is striking in its simplicity, and it has universal appeal. This begins with six-year-old Christopher Albert and carries all the way to our elders, Mrs. Josephine Hood, the mother of 17 adult children, and Mrs. Marian McCollum. *Legacy* was written to the African-American adolescents in my high school's mentoring program in the hopes of awakening them to the legacy granted to them by their ancestors; however, *Legacy*, like all of this wisdom, is for those who are open to receiving it.

Conversations with the Divine have been included exactly as they occurred. He first spoke to me as an answer to my prayers in my twenties. I said, "I need a sign, but You know me. I'm blind! So I need it in big neon letters!" He responded in the big, booming Moses-and-the-burning-bush voice. He was concise, and I got the message. He spoke to me a few more times over the years, but conversations began in earnest during the writing of this book starting with *The Divine Calls Us to Love.* Believe me when I say that I was stunned and amazed that first time and the times that followed! Looking back, He has spoken quietly to me throughout my life; however, I just called it my Spirit. The Divine speaks to you as well. He invites you to return to You, to *be* in the world as a physical manifestation of Him, and to love as He does. Every moment can be a spiritual practice and is an opportunity to *be* connected to Him all of the time, to know Eternity all of the time. Heaven abounds in you! This is an invitation to live in the fullness granted to You by the Divine.

Namasté,
Balin A. Durr, M.D.

Prelude to the Journey

1

He Is…We Are

The Creator of all that is has many names as we are many people. This includes the One, the Divine, God, Source, Universal Consciousness, Higher Self, Universal Wisdom, Buddha, Life, Allah, Atman, I Am, Eternity, Beloved, and many others. Some are used interchangeably, but I like calling Him the Divine because it reminds me of His magnificence and our Divinity.

He is the morning sunrise and the evening sunset. He is the desert sands and the world's vast oceans. He is the sweet twitter of a bird; the thick, luscious green grass; and the hypnotic savannahs of the motherland. He is everything that we can think of and that which is yet to be revealed. There is no place where He is not and nowhere He has not been. Stretch your hand outward, and He is there. Journey to the stars, and see Him twinkling at you. He creates with infinite vision. His splendor is unbounded and will carry you where He wills it even unto the corners of Forever.

His depth surpasses man's known reach, and His heights stretch beyond the farthest reaches of every imagination. All at once, He is one and He is billions. There is nothing that He is not because He is everything and everyone including you. He is the beggar and the inch worm. He is the prince and the king of the pride. Everywhere you turn, you see His likeness and creations. Everywhere you turn, you see Him.

Who are you? You are Him—That which He created as an expression of Himself to be like Him. You embody all that He is! He is eternal as are you. If you are wondering, "How can I Be Him?" Easily! The same way the ocean can be the Ocean. When you start with an Ocean and scoop a cup of ocean water out, that water is still the Ocean even though it's a smaller, separated amount. It has all of the properties and contents of the larger body. You are the cup of ocean that remains the Ocean. You are Him in compact form.

Since we are Him, our Divine energy has many names just as He does. Our Divinity is called the Soul, Spirit, Divine Self, True Self, Authentic Self, and Being along with others. Prior to coming into the world, we were One with the Divine and all that is. The world of Spirit is referred to as formless or unmanifest. The physical world is form or the manifestation of formless. We existed as energy without form when we were One with the Divine. Now we exist as energy in form, also known as a body, and we return to formless when the body dies. So everything is energy whether it is formless or in form, and energy in the physical realm can exist in different states. Think of water, which can exist as ice, liquid, or vapor. There is a perpetual cycle of energy moving back and forth between formless and form, between unmanifest and manifest, because energy cannot be created nor destroyed. This is transformation—the changing of form. Once our tasks are complete, the body dies and returns to the Earth; but the immortal Soul or Spirit returns to formless once again. So that which is truly You never dies. It just moves in and out of form. You transform!

Another important characteristic of energy is that it vibrates at various frequencies and draws other energy to it that has the same frequency. It's like being on a conference call. Everyone calls the same number and enters their password. Only those parties with the correct password can hear and be heard on the same call. This is being on the same frequency. So every thought, word, and deed has a frequency and attracts people and events on the same frequency. This is also known as the Law of Attraction. This can occur in a conscious or unconscious way.

So why did You leave formless to come into form, the manifest, or a body? You did this so that your Divine Self could experience itself and others on this plane. You are Spirit that has come here to have a human experience. You know this early on in life. It is the way of a child that embodies the Divine, but living causes you to gradually forget that your essence is an eternal Soul. You believe you are the human experience you've undertaken in the body, but you are not! Pierre Teilhard de Chardin said, "We are not human beings having a spiritual experience; we are spiritual beings having a human experience."[3] Let me repeat that. You are a spiritual being that has come to the Earth to experience your Self in human form. You are NOT a human being that decided to be spiritual! You could only know or experience your Self as Spirit, Soul, or Divine Self if you experience your Self as something else; in this case, as human. You have to know who you are not in order to know who You are. If everyone was in the formless state, You wouldn't recognize who You are because it would all *be* the same, and there would *be* nothing different to compare your Self to. When you take on your human form, everything seems different. So there is much to compare your Self to, and this facilitates the remembrance of who You are. The same dynamic is played out in many other ways as well. There is hot and cold, light and dark, hard and soft, and good and evil. Opposites allow us to know the other and ourselves.

Until knowingness returns, many also believe we are different from others. This is the ultimate misperception. We are really all One, all the same, but we wear different clothing or disguises. The difference is only superficial and is meant to be a signpost, but most of us confuse the disguise or clothing with ourselves. The superficial differences or disguises include variations in physical appearance, nationality, socio-economic status, and belief systems. We believe that our True Self is the clothing or disguise, and we believe the same about other people. We then believe we are different from them, and the more "other" they are, the more of an enemy they become. We then believe we can do all kinds of things to them including taking their life.

They are not the other, and we are not different. We are all One with the Divine. Believing that we are separate or different in any meaningful way would be the same as saying that your right foot belonged to someone else just because you put a different sock on it. The Divine created us in His likeness. So we are all Him and are One with Him. There is no separation from Him or others. Knowing Him and your Self as Him is returning Home. When you understand and know this, you are aligned with Him, have access to Universal Wisdom, and co-create with Him and like Him. Unity with Him means You see your Self in the face of others and in nature. You see You everywhere, knowing that what You really see everywhere is the One. Remembrance of our Oneness is the journey we must all take. This is the purpose of the journey in the physical form. You get to choose You in every moment, in every choice, then you get to do it all over once again. This journey is the path back to Spirit, back to Him. This is the path of the One to the One.

2

Tapestry

We are all part of the grand web of Life, connected by shimmering gossamer strands that pass to and through every Being and entity. The strands are interwoven like the threads of a fine tapestry. It is a rich tapestry infused with a kaleidoscope of colors, eye-catching details, and a variety of textures and yarns woven into an intricate pattern that invite you to run your hand across the cloth. This is artistry at its finest—crafted by skilled, seasoned, intensely creative hands that seem to bring the tapestry to Life. The beauty of it speaks to you, seeming to know your name. It envelops you, wrapping you in its comfort and warmth.

How can this be happening? You don't seem to know. It is a tapestry not a blanket, but it is Life's tapestry. Here, all things are possible and exist along the strands; all connected One to another One. They surround and bind us One to the other. Giving what needs to be given. Providing what needs to be provided. Nourishing what needs nourishment. The strands seem tenuous and fragile but are deceptively strong and ever present. As a strand is stretched or moved, so too do the others. Their flexibility allows them to bend and stretch, to flex and give. It happens in concert. When a tear is left, it too is born by the others. A repair is made, but the tapestry is irrevocably altered. Yet, it is resilient and strong, buoyed by its connection to the others. It is a grand design meant to survive the ages, and it does. In doing so, it allows any Being and entity to do so as well.

This tapestry connects Life to Itself because everything is connected. We are all One with the Divine and are all connected to each other. It can *be* no other way. The energy of all Beings is ever present, but it is only when we still our minds that we sense their presence. What does this tell us? Many things, if we are willing to hear. This life and Life speaks to us all of the time. Sometimes it speaks in a soft whisper. Sometimes it speaks in the big, booming Moses-and-the-burning-bush voice! No matter the volume, the connection between all Beings is your ally and serves you as you serve others. It is imperative that you make choices consciously because the consequences affect you and others, sometimes in sweeping and unanticipated ways. You cannot harm another without being harmed yourself just as you cannot love another without being loved yourself.

We share the same energy vibration as someone we feel connected to when we focus our attention on seeing or speaking to them. Our energy vibrates along these strands—intersecting, interacting, and rippling outward like a pebble tossed upon the water. It is invisible to the eye until the manifestation appears before us like a magic spell cast by a powerful, enchanted Being.

These strands of Life enable us to call others to us as well as things and events even in our unawareness. Someone will call us by phone, they'll show up on our doorstep, or we "just happen" to see them during an outing. They are responding to the call that was broadcasted in the universe.

This connection also means that no One is ever alone or ever has to go without because it is all there within the tapestry. Feeling alone and deprived means you have disconnected from the Universal Force that provides and is everything. "I Am That I Am. I Am all That Is," He said.[4] Disconnecting causes suffering, which ends when you reconnect. Find your connection in stillness. Find it in nature. Find it all about you because the Divine is all around you and always with you.

Just call to it. Just call to Life. We are all One Body. We are all connected.

3

Scarcity/Abundance

Many believe scarcity is about the lack of resources, restrictive limitations, and unmet needs and wants. People win and lose at the expense of others. This is used to justify all kinds of behavior including the taking of precious life. Real scarcity is a belief that you are not enough and are undeserving. There can't possibly be enough of all that you want in the Universe if you are not enough. How could there be? And even if there were, someone else deserves it more. If you question whether this holds true for you, ask yourself, "Am I willing to tell myself the truth about who I am and what I want, and am I willing to tell others that same truth?" Answering "no" means you fear that you are unacceptable as you are and what you want will not be granted to you. This is a belief rooted in fear. It's a fear that ripples through your consciousness and permeates your existence. It haunts you like the starving child, who never knows when he'll eat again. Those large, vacant eyes and sunken cheeks convey the pain of a bloated emptiness that gnaws away at your insides. You hope it will pass, but it's an aching hunger that never seems to dissipate.

You look to the world instead of looking to Him and your Self in your efforts to assuage your hunger and fear. Anything outside of you is temporary and will pass away from existence. Careers come and go. Beauty and health fade. A car rusts and falls into disrepair. A building decays and turns to rubble. A civilization reaches its pinnacle then ebbs from memory except as a notation in history books. What happens to your sense of self when you lose your job, your mate leaves, the car gets repossessed, or the house goes into foreclosure? It crumbles if it is grounded in such transient things. You will never be permanently satiated by something that has a beginning and an end, and every THING does!

Feelings of scarcity bring about separation from the Divine. You believe the Divine will not provide all that you need and hope for. This means going without. Ultimately, you fear going without love. In your darkest hour, it means going without His love. How many times did you compromise or settle for something that wasn't even close to what you wanted because you believed you couldn't have your true heart's desire? How many dreams did you allow to fester in the smoldering, sunbaked heat of your disbelief? What did you relinquish, throw away, or surrender so that you could get what you thought would never come again? Was it your time, honor, dignity, integrity, money, health, or humanity? Oftentimes, it was our self that lay torn and tattered—a semblance of a long held idea.

True abundance is rooted in Spirit, in knowing who You really are, and that everything is One with the Divine. It stems from Being, which is eternal. Everything exists in the formless first then comes into form or Being through an idea and the work of the believer. Everything is available to everyone at any given time because we live in a Universe of abundance, and the Divine is all there is. So, why does it appear otherwise? Wayne Dyer said, "I will attract into my life what I am and not what I want."[5] This is a reflection of who you believe yourself to be. Can you let go of what you fear losing? Instead, grab hold of the infinite possibilities and creativity in the Universe and in You! What you sought was always within You because the Divine resides within You. You can manifest anything in every moment. It's just waiting for you to breathe life into it. SWOOOOOOO!

Abundance allows us to manifest love, peace, joy, contentment, prosperity, and health in any moment in spite of any external experience because they reside within us. We bring our feelings to the moment, not the other way around. The moment or event does NOT bring them to us. It may seem that a person or event brings them to us, but we decide if we'll respond with joy and excitement, dismay, or not at all. Our emotional response is always our choice. Choose consciously!

When you choose to be open and connected to all that is, Life flows freely through you. Your sense of well-being, and that you are more than enough because you too are infinite, emanates from this space. Well-being means our Being is well! Many don't seem to know this, don't seem to know their Being, or that they are Being. Therefore, they don't know themselves. We miss out on all that we truly are because we don't recognize ourselves as that glorious and wonderful creation of the Divine come here to *be* in the world and to show others how to *be* here too! Come from a place of Being, not as our mind and thoughts tell us to do it, but as our Being guides us to do it. Be in the world!

Living life with an open hand and heart means living from a place of abundance. You give freely to others knowing that you have it to give, and that it will be given to you because of your generous nature. Let it flow from you like the waters of the mighty Mississippi. If you'd like friendship, love, or prosperity and don't believe you have it, give it away anyway! Someone always has less than you. By giving it away, you'll learn that you always had it within you.

Abundance is also about trust. Trust that what you need to get you from moment to moment, from day to day, is present or will show up! If you doubt that, look at all of the days behind you. If what you needed in the past was absent, you would not be here today. Trust that the Divine in His Universal Wisdom will know what you need and ensure that it is granted to you when He knows that it will serve you best. It's about trust. Trust that the Divine, the Universe, and You are everything. There can be no scarcity in that.

The Journey

4

Storms

Have you ever gone out to play in the rain? Remember the gentle feel of the water as it caressed your skin and hit your tongue, the pitter patter as it fell upon the sidewalk and against the window pane, the sweet smell of grass in the spring? The children giggled with delight as they gleefully jumped up and down in puddles. Remember the feelings of peace and contentment that filled your Being as you soaked it all in? There was a quiet beauty that seemed to blanket everything despite the grey overcast sky. Time could have stood still, and you would have happily spent eternity in that moment.

Then came that first sharp crackle of lightning followed closely by the deafening boom of thunder, and everyone scrambled for shelter! Once safely inside, though, you felt compelled to watch this churning, tumultuous force of nature. The water ran down the window in sheets and down the street as if chased by some ethereal specter. Electricity was in the air creating an eerie glow. Again, you were grateful for shelter that allowed you to see this from a safe distance.

Now imagine that this is your life! Times of quiet beauty intermingled with torrential downpours. They may be nudges or shatter the very foundation. Everyone has experienced some type of storm. It may be a fender bender, financial trouble, job loss, cancer, physical or sexual abuse, a baby left in a dumpster, an earthquake, or genocide.

How would we truly know who we are without the storms? They challenge us to evolve, to elevate, and to reach deep within where we find pools of strength, resolve, and our own brilliance. They remind us that we are Spirits who have come to the Earth School to have human experiences but are not bound by them. The storms are there to help us transcend, to remind us that we are in the world but not of it. We are not meant to become entrenched or mired down by the storms, stuck like a needle on an old record player. We are meant to learn the life lesson, overcome, and continue on our path. Dr. Michael Bernard Beckwith said delays bring forth gifts that we need to take with us on the journey.[6] Unfortunately, people tend to make these challenging times a part of their identity especially if they were traumatic. While those experiences happened to you, they are not you. Yes, they shape you. Yes, you have become the person that you are today because of them, but who You truly are exists separate and apart from your experiences. The true essence of our Being is an immortal Soul.

Once you get this in your core, you can create distance between you and any event so that you can see it for what it is—just something that happened. See it as an opportunity to learn or heal. It's the difference between viewing a tree up close or viewing the whole forest from a hilltop. Now you can fully appreciate its majesty including your place in it.

So don't avoid or just endure storms. Embrace the storms! Marvel at their beauty! Feel the electrical charge! Admire the magnificence and splendor of the brilliant flash of lightning and the gigantic boom of the thunder. See the holiness in all people, things, and the process. You will have embraced the holiness of the process when you embrace the storms along with the quiet beauty of the gentler times.

5

Loss

We are infinite Souls temporarily expressed as human beings. Every Soul has a purpose and departs once that purpose is fulfilled. Their time here may be for hours or decades. When the time comes for your loved One to leave this plane, you will continue to have that which matters most—your connection and their love. We remain connected to those who have returned to their formless state because everything is connected to and through the Divine. You are connected with them beyond the five senses once they leave the body. It is our conceptualization that causes us to believe that we have "lost" someone. When in actuality, it is we who have lost our knowing. They are always with us. This connection is limitless just as you are. Death is not an end but a return to formless Eternity. We transform from Spirit to the body and back to Spirit many times. We are eternal!

If your loved one's time on this plane is coming to an end, do not fret or worry. That is a future moment. It has not occurred, and worry renders you unavailable to make the most of NOW. You miss the opportunity to love, to celebrate, to have joy in the only moment you ever have at any time. You also stress your Being with negative energy, and you need all of your resources to continue being a powerful, creative force in the universe and to support your loved one as they approach their transition. Our greatest legacy is found in those that we've loved and those who've loved us. So *be* at ease, my friend. Live, love, laugh, and celebrate the wonder of Life in the only moment we ever have—Now!

6

From the Center of Being

There is a stillness deep within you that connects you to the Center of Creation and all that is. Let that center of Being guide you as you move through your day. It is here where peace resides despite the multitude of demands tugging at you simultaneously, and it is from here where you can be like a leaf floating on the swirling winds of Eternity.

7

Can You Come Sit with Me?

It was a call from the center of my Being, from the Divine. There was an ease to it. It was warm, inviting, and had a subtle underlying longing that told me of its sincerity. The resistance that had existed due to fear had faded, and I could say yes. I could accept the invitation that called to me softly these many years. It was to be with Myself, not the self defined by the world, but the Self that was Divine and with the Divine. It was to be at peace, to be joyful, to just Be.

8

Emptied Out

Misery so enormous,
So overwhelming,
It filled every fiber.
It oozed from every pore.
There was no room for anything else.
No room for me,
Only room for misery.
The tears welled up,
And overflowed the banks.
Overtaken by anguish,
Taken over once more.
Desolation was my playground,
Despair my playmate.
Curled into a ball
By the agony of it all.
This was no herbivore,
A carnivore for sure.
I had filled up to the point
Where I had emptied out,
Flashed the VACANCY sign.

9

Don't Answer to Mess

"It ain't what people call you. It's what you answer to." [7]

~ *Tyler Perry*

What I love about young children is that they remind me most of what the Divine is like. I feel and experience their God Consciousness in so many of their ways: joy, spontaneity, beauty, creativity, and love. Over time, the world chips away at the memory of their True Self until they can only recall a remnant of it. They began to think they are only human instead of Spirit having a human experience. This is unconsciousness. We know that unconscious people can say cruel things, and this begins in childhood. These callous insults damage confidence and erode fragile self-esteem. We often believe the derogatory barbs especially if our light giving presence is not being affirmed, and even when it is, this harmful chatter can overwhelm and drown out the affirmations that become just so much background noise to the cacophony of dribble that wounds our tender heart.

The Divine granted me the splendid gift of healing. The blessing in this is that helping others often means helping myself. Working with children often evokes memories of my own childhood, and I feel a kinship with many of them. I easily recalled the pain I felt as "my kids" recounted their experiences of rejection at the hands of their uncaring counterparts. Wounds were torn open by malicious jabs and were slow to heal as evidenced by the anguish on the faces of the young storytellers. Many of us have endured this. Children seem to find and exploit everyone's weaknesses, but if you don't know this, you are left feeling alone, isolated, embattled, and beleaguered.

How could I get them to see that this was an experience shared by many and, more importantly, your sense of self does not have to be defined by others? We each get to decide what we are going to answer to. Then it came to me. I was seeing Laila*, and she, like many others, was depressed and unhappy with herself because she didn't fit the very narrow definition of beauty in this country. It was alarming that this was manifesting as cutting on herself.

I asked, "What if I called you Nicole? Would you answer?"

"No," she said.

"Why not?"

"That's not my name."

"What if I called you Lauren or Mary? Would you answer?"

_____
*The name was changed to maintain anonymity.

Again she replied, "No."

"Why not?"

"That's not my name."

"What if I called you James? Would you answer?"

"No," she stated.

"Why not?"

This time she responded with a bit of exasperation in her voice. "Because it's not my name!"

"So why are you are answering to that other mess?"

I could see the light bulb go off! She knew that just as she didn't answer to being called Nicole, Mary, or James because they are not who she is, she didn't have to feel hurt by the insults that others called her because that wasn't who she was either. She understood that she was the one who ultimately decided who she was and others' characterizations of her didn't have to define her reality. In other words, she didn't have to answer to that mess!

What occurred to me in that same moment was neither did I. I am an expression of the Divine and all that that embodies regardless of what others expected of or thought about me. A large weight had been lifted from me, and I felt liberated! What also occurred to me is that many adults still carry the burdens and wounds inflicted upon them because their sense of their

Divine Self is a distant, fleeting shadow. Your True Self beckons and invites you to remember.

You are an expression of the Divine—magnificent and holy, powerfully creative, and yes, emotional! You embody the Divine's best! Know this. Own this. Be guided by this in all that you manifest. Do not allow the rest of the world to tell you who you are because in their unconsciousness, they too have forgotten this about themselves. As Jesus said, "...they know not what they do."[8] So follow that which calls you to manifest your magnificence in every day, in every moment.

10

The Fullness of the Divine

Wherever you are, there too is the fullness of the Divine. That means that You too are full already, complete already, because You are an expression of the Divine. There is nothing you need to repair, do, or be except your Divine Self. The perfection lies in our Being, in our Divine Self, not in our humanness. It is our human self that falters. In your Oneness with the Divine, you co-create your life daily. You already have infinite possibilities within you waiting to be expressed. The difference between everyone else and "successful" people is that the latter believe in their ability to take a possibility and manifest it in the physical world. Isn't it time to manifest the gifts that are the reason for your presence in this place at this time? All that awaits is a shift in consciousness, an awareness of who You really are, the recognition of your Divinely given gifts, and your manifestation of them in your own unique and special way. Will you step into your fullness today?

11

Darling

My darling and a darling,
Rare and special.
So unaware of how you ripple and flow
Through the lives of those around you.
You are love in a myriad of colors and waves.
Gently lapping against the ear lobe, shoulder, senses.

12

360 Degrees

Beware of the mind and its incessant chatter. It intends to be protective, helpful. But in the end, it can be treacherous—a place of steamy swamps, smelly bogs, and man-eating plants from which there may be no escape! This is being stuck in your head, which is in stark contrast to coming from a place of Being. This offers stillness, clarity. You can "see" Heaven and Earth, time in motion, time in 360 degrees. There is no past, present, or future because they all exist simultaneously in 360 degrees if one has the "eyes" to see. It's just one stream of Consciousness. Being knows it as this, but the mind can only perceive it linearly— one occurrence at a time—and in limited shades of grey. Our existence is multidimensional and layered like a 20-tiered chess game.

13

Space

I am not alone. I am with myself, who works to have the courage to be patient until the one who is for me appears. I see the blessing in my male friends who have loved me, nurtured me, and allowed me to do the healing work that I needed to do these past years. The true miracle is that I see the blessing in those who withheld from me as well. Somehow a space was created for something unexpected to take root and flourish because others refrained from granting me that which I sought, expected, and desperately wanted at times. I feel that space now, the openness of it, and the contentment of allowing it to be as it is. There's no urgency to fill it, no desire to make it into something else. That space just seems to fill me, and in this moment, that is more than enough.

14

Expectations

A dear friend of mine once said that he had no expectations for relationships outside of work. I thought, "Huh, that's different. I just need to sit with this," as my mind began to grapple with what I had just heard. It wasn't that I didn't understand because I did. I just hadn't thought of it that way. I also knew that some people would think that he had no standards. He had standards, but what he didn't have were expectations that people meet those standards outside of a work environment. I understood what he was saying and knew this lesson was vital. Yet, I was trapped in the quicksand of an intellect that could barely grasp the branch extended to me as a lifeline. Everyone knows that struggling in quicksand leads to your rapid submersion and demise, but I continued to struggle greatly with this notion. I just couldn't seem to get it. Then one day that changed.

No one can ever be everything that others expect when they expect it. Nor do we even want to be, but we seem to want this from others. I began to see that we are all on our own path with our own lessons to learn in our own time. Oprah said,

"First you get a whisper, then a tap on the shoulder, then a slap upside the head, and then the brick wall falls on you." Each of us has to decide when to answer the call to become more of our Divine Self. Having expectations for others doesn't allow for this, doesn't allow for each other's individuality, and suggests that we know what's best for someone else. Our intentions may come from wanting our own needs met or from a place of wanting what's best for someone else. We want them to avoid painful and difficult times. We want them to avoid the mistakes we made, but we don't know how their pain might become someone else's salvation.

However, we add to their suffering and our own by failing to allow them to make their own journey. This is especially true when their consciousness is not prepared to learn what we desire to teach them and is not prepared to evolve at the pace that we insist upon. We need to allow for the fact that we can't always see the big picture. We don't know how their life lessons will serve them and humanity. It is incumbent upon us to be compassionate and patient, to honor them and the process, and to allow what will be anyway. Then ask yourself, "How can I give to myself and the Universe what I expected from others?" Therein lies the fundamental quest for us all. How can I be more of myself instead of expecting others to be that which I may not have been either?

15

Parents' Gift

Most of us would've liked more from our parents, or as a wise Soul, Marian McCollum, told me, we "would like a better brush" of them. We wanted more of their time, compassion, guidance, support, and, yes, more of their love. We wanted to feel that we mattered and were more important than whatever or whomever they were chasing in order to ease their demons and fill those hungry, empty spaces. We wanted them to recognize us as the vibrant, amazing gifts that were placed in their care to nurture and shepherd through this life. Some children got much of this while others got a nightmare. Some got a lot of stuff and not much else. While others got only a modest amount of stuff but got a whole lot of love. Whatever we got from our parents, they gave us what they had based upon their level of consciousness and what had been given to them. You give love if it was given to you. You give chaos and despair if that was given to you as well. A sapling cannot bear fruit and a five year old cannot bear children because she has not developed the ability. The capacity exists, but it will only be expressed with maturation and evolvement.

Could our parents have done better? Yes, but that was their best at that moment given their life experiences and their recognition and willingness to be a gentler, kinder, more effective parent. Our parents' basic and fundamental task is to give us life so that we can manifest our magnificence in the world. Some come together solely for this purpose, then continue on separate paths.

Our task is to take whatever was given, develop ourselves, and express that magnificence. We are so much more than what our parents gave or withheld from us. We too develop more to give than was given to us when consciousness evolves and recognizes that we are not limited by our circumstances because we are infinite Spirits and boundless. Failure to recognize this keeps us stuck, tied to limitations, and focused on our frailties instead of our possibilities. T.D. Jakes said we should be grateful for what others didn't give us.[9] Why? Because it gives us the opportunity to evolve and learn life lessons that may not have occurred otherwise. We learn forgiveness, compassion, and to be open to receiving love from whomsoever gives it to us. Love is not bound by blood lines or biology. Love is given to those with an open heart.

So it doesn't matter where you started, how far in the back of the pack you came from, or what happened along the way. What you created while you were here is all that matters when it's said and done. Did you manifest your Divine gifts? Know that some parents give their children much and some give little, but all parents give their children life. There is much to be grateful for in that single gift.

16

Loving

Relationships are mirrors. They reflect who we are because we call people to us who vibrate on the same frequency. They reflect the light and the dark, our magnificence and our woundedness. Our Divine Self is reflected in the light, and the dark offers the most opportunity for healing. Relationships are here to teach us about ourselves for whatever period of time or number of seasons they remain with us.

Fortunately, I began to call loved ones these past few years that reflected the light and taught me about loving in ways that I could only hope were true because that had not been my experience to a large extent. I saw loving as a gentle, tender expression of oneness and union, but my experience was more like a physical contest between combatants who pummel each other. The winner emerges victorious but bruised and battered— an emotional shard that is beautiful to look at but treacherous and life stealing as it slices and disembowels its next "love."

There is much we call love that has nothing to do with love. We watch others struggle, suffer, and endure indignities in the name of what they call love. Worse yet, we emulate what we've seen. This is not love. Love honors us, serves and nurtures us, and is uplifting. If it does not do this, it needs another name. Is this an opportunity to heal and a life lesson about what love is not? Yes. Is it something to avoid in the future? Yes. But this is not love—the ultimate expression of the Divine.

As my consciousness shifted, more light was reflected by those who appeared. They reflected back to me my own magnificence when I was adrift in the darkness. They were lighthouses, shining beacons, giving light where there had been none for a long time. The gift was that I got to see myself through their loving, adoring eyes. Love and affirmations were poured upon me, which was a balm to my wounded heart. I saw myself in ways that were previously unprecedented, unrealized and unappreciated—beautiful, wonderful, and a blessing to others. This was a gentle, balmy breeze that lifted me to the heavens, and I soared! At the same time, it was like a cool mountain stream— soothing, healing, and life giving. I took flight and remained grounded all at the same time. This was love that was free, deep, and wondrous. I feel it as I feel my breath, as I feel my heartbeat, as I feel connected to the Center of Creation. The joy in my heart overflows, and I can't help but laugh! I released insecurities and came to appreciate and value the fullness of my Being. There was no need to fear the loss or absence of loved ones because I embodied the very characteristics that I admired in them, and the infinite creativity of the Divine meant there would be others. It is my heart that knows, that reassures my head when it starts to doubt. This is a journey that spans time and space, and what I have gained is immeasurable whether my loved ones remained with me for a moment, a year, or a lifetime.

Of course, the real measure of any life lesson is to take what's been learned, become self-sustaining, and then pass it on to others. Loving ourselves and others is what our Divine Self calls us to do even when our behavior is at its most unlovable. So it is with honor and deep gratitude that I acknowledge my extraordinary loved ones who've taken this journey with me and taught me about loving myself, loving others, and the magic of two joined Souls.

17

The Divine Calls Us to Love

Hi! I am Home, back to the One who loved me first, who loved me always. You allowed me to breathe. You allowed me to Be. You just allowed. I didn't always know that You were there, but You were. I see that now. I know this for certain. How my heart rejoices in Your Presence. How I smile at the thought of You. You are magic, and the Universe delights in Your infinity. Oh, how I longed for You even when I did not know that it was You. Joy abounds, and Your love is in and of everything. Always seeking, seeking that which most don't seem to know. Ah, but wait. There is light. There is You.

"Who? you ask. But you already know even if you cannot give it a name. Why? Because I have called to you these many years. You've heard the voice, softly at times, urgently at others. It was the voice of Love. What else would you call Me? Many call Me by many names, but ultimately, it is One."

"One?"

"Yes, One. It is all One regardless of how it may appear."

"But One what?"

"Just One. One Love. How else could it be? You would have it be many, be separate, but that is not My way. My way 'Is that I am.' Do you hear it calling? Do you feel it calling? It calls you to love as the One, One as the Divine, One with the Divine, One as the Divine. There is no separation, just One, just Love, just Divinity, just Sacred. Here you go. There you go. Just go with Me. It's a place you already know. It's a place you've already been. It's time to return Home. It's time to return to Love. It's time to return to Me. Do you remember? Yes, I can see that you do. Yes, that's how Home feels. My love was always with you. Now it's time for you to give it away, to share it with others. I will help you. I have always helped you. Remember? Yes, I see that you do. And I will help you again. Know that always. Always and into infinity, even when you return Home and go back again. Yes, I will always help you. So breathe a sigh of relief because I know that you want to. It's a sigh born of doubt and alleviated by a relief in knowing of My Eternal Presence. On Me, you can depend. Now go to sleep, and rest easily in the knowledge that I am always here and always loving you. Smile and sweet dreams, My child."

18

Legacy

"Your crown has been bought and paid for.
All you must do is put it on your head."

~ *James Baldwin*

I come before you out of love and with humility. My heart calls to your heart in hopes that you are open to hearing the trumpet sound that calls you to awaken—to awaken to who you are, to who you have been, and to who you will become. I believe in your future, and I am concerned about it as well. There is a malaise that is pervasive and eats away at our existence like a cancer. Our children don't know who they are and seem to have no sense of where they came from. There is no sense of legacy, that magnificent gift granted to you by your ancestors, who survived the transatlantic crossing chained to each other, lying in their own urine and feces, denigration, the stripping of their names and culture, and attempts to deny their humanity. These were people who picked cotton, did others' laundry, swept floors, cleaned toilets, and were porters. They endured discrimination, beatings, amputations and lynching. They fought, struggled, and died so that you—their offspring, their future—would have life. But somehow, their sacrifices seem a distant memory to many and irrelevant to others as we've taken on the values of a society that values profit above everything else including human beings and life, especially those belonging to people of color.

We come from a continent of people who were connected to the creative force in the Universe and understood that everything was sacred and had a purpose. They understood their place in the flow of life and that everything was connected. Community was central, and the well-being of the individual and community was intertwined. They respected wisdom that was earned from experience and time on this plane. There were kings and queens who were highly revered rulers and brilliant strategists. It was a land of high culture, intricate political systems, music, religion, architecture, science and math, whose influence is seen throughout the world today.

Despite all of this, there are those that still continue to deny the importance and pervasiveness of this legacy and deny your worth and meaningfulness. What's more tragic is our failure to recognize it in ourselves. You are beautiful and brilliant, gifted and anointed by the Creator of all that is. You have more to offer the world than just your looks, your athletic ability, what money you earn, or bearing children that you don't know how to love, nurture, or parent. To the girls: you are regal, majestic, creative, and an expression of the cradle of life on this planet. To the boys: you are strong modern warriors and majestic in your own right.

You are the providers and protectors of your family, and our survival depends upon you. Why do you think you are under attack on so many levels? There is a reason why so many of you are uneducated, unemployed, and out of the home. There is a reason why your women are allowed some success and you are made to perish. It is because you are in competition with the dominant culture for all of the resources: power, influence, money, jobs, and mates.

Both of you are thinkers, philosophers, and emotional beings as well. You have a future that's meaningful and bright regardless of those who tell you that, "you don't do nothing, don't contribute nothing, and ain't worth nothing." This is not your heritage nor should it be your legacy. Somehow, this internalized self-hatred from the society has turned into an insidious, rancid sickness that says it's okay to be mediocre and to do little more than exist. You were not put here to just breathe, exist, and suck up resources. You are more than an athletic gladiator that entertains the masses. You weren't meant to fill prison cells, drug houses, and cemeteries. Your children weren't meant to be neglected and abused. You weren't meant to be the subject on the nightly news as another shooting victim. Our ancestors weep at how we've lost our way and demand that we return to that which is our inheritance and birthright. Your legacy is one of greatness and calls to you to wake up!

Everyone on the planet has a purpose. Your primary purpose is to awaken and live life consciously. You must understand that every thought and action has a consequence. Living life consciously means that you have thought about those possible consequences prior to choosing and are willing to live with them whatever they are. For example, if you decide to have unprotected sex, you are willing to become a parent and/or contract a sexually transmitted infection. Living life consciously means you don't continue to make the same choices and fail to understand why the results are the same (e.g., I have three children because I didn't use contraception.). The alternative is I want to go to college and have a career before starting a family. So I will either wait to have sex or use contraception during sex.

Another example would be what kind of choices do you make when you feel pressured by others to act like you aren't smart, skip class, use drugs, or break the law? Do you examine the impact upon your future when you choose to go along with your peers? These decisions will determine the type and number of options you will have for a career. Do you make decisions that undermine your education and preparation or do you make decisions that have you positioned well for advancement in your chosen career? Professions involve a mixture of reasoning abilities and labor. Some require more use of your intellect while others require more brawn. It doesn't matter what type of work you do as long as it's honorable and you are passionate about it. You want your profession to be one that you chose, not one you settled for because you were ill-prepared and had few alternatives. The decisions you make now will determine whether you make your money with your head or your back. It is imperative that you choose consciously!

Your secondary purpose is to manifest your gifts. You have a gift that's rare and special and will be expressed in a way that's uniquely your own. You sense this on some level. As our children, you are our love and our light. Those adults who know this about themselves know this about you. We recognize our own light. So we recognize yours as well. There are those who don't know this about themselves. So they are unable to recognize it in you. You must gain clarity about your gift, about your purpose. It is your purpose along with intention that guides and directs your choices and gives shape to the outcome. It's like wandering the desert when one is without purpose. It's like trying to see your reflection in a moving stream when you lack clarity of purpose. At its worse, you get mud—thick, goopy, dirty, blinding, messy results because you were unclear about what you sought to create. Your challenge is to manifest your gift, your purpose, regardless of the challenges and in spite of those who don't see your value.

Now you must understand that there will be those who don't understand your purpose and others who will ridicule it and you. Do not dumb yourself down in order to fit in and be accepted. You must have the strength of character and purpose to follow your own path. Maya Angelou speaks of the ancestors surrounding us during great challenges and when we are called upon to be our best. You stand on the shoulders of your ancestors, and you have a responsibility to them, yourselves, and those who come after you to live life in a way that is a light unto others and builds a bridge to the future instead of one that leads to more hopelessness and despair. Every one of you has brilliance and greatness! Others may not get your value. That's okay. It doesn't mean you have no value. It means they have no vision.

Now something else to consider is this: who do you hang out with? If you want to know who you are, look at your peer group, the people you give your time to. If they are thugs, you are a thug. If they are pot heads, you are a pot head. If they are smart and successful, you are smart and successful, and if you are the smartest one in your group, then you need a new group. Why? Because you want to be with others who challenge and encourage you to grow beyond the person you are today.

"How do I determine my purpose?" you ask. You must learn to quiet your mind by meditating daily and be willing to hear the answers to the following questions: "Who am I? What is my purpose? Why am I here? What am I called to do?" Listen to your intuitive Self, that part of you that is connected to all that is and imparts wisdom and guidance. Be patient as you wait to hear the answers because they may not come quickly, but they will come. Pointers to the answers include feelings of excitement, exhilaration, and joy about what you do! You are passionate about your work and could do it all day. This is being in the flow. This is bliss. As you travel your path, ask yourself, "Do my choices and my way of Being in the world honor and serve my purpose and the greater good?" The way we live our lives is a lesson for others. It can be either a warning or an example.

Whatever your gift or purpose, know that you will have to work for it. Success is earned for most. It is not just given to them, and everyone experiences adversity. People spend years and thousands of hours preparing for success. Forest Whitaker's character in the movie, "The Great Debaters" said, "They must do what they have to do in order to do what they want to do."[10] Successful people are disciplined, focused, make sacrifices, and have faith in themselves and their gifts. They are determined to overcome challenges and setbacks including unemployment and homelessness, and, most importantly, they never, ever give up! These are the times that determine character. Character is built during the difficult times, not the good times. It is forged in the fire and pressure of the crucible called life. It is tested in the valley not on the mountaintop. So hold fast, and do not surrender!

Ultimately, your success will be determined by your way of Being in the world. Who did you love and who loved you? If you had children, were they happy and whole? Did you make a difference in the lives of those you encountered while you were here? Is humanity better off because of your presence on the planet? Were you a light in the darkness? Rev. Martin Luther King, Jr. said, "Everyone can be great...because everyone can serve." How did you use your gifts to serve others?

My beloved young Ones, this is a call to awaken—to awaken to who you really are, and to awaken to your unique purpose on this planet. We are a people who've wandered the desert for centuries, but through you, we can become a flourishing oasis once again. Your ancestors are your foundation and strength, but you are our future, our aspirations, our hope expressed as living, breathing Beings in flight. We have faith in you and the greatness inherent within you because it was given to you in your DNA, and, more importantly, it resides within your heart. So when you look back upon your life, what will your legacy be? Will it be a cautionary tale of warning or a shining example for others to follow?

19

There Is Only Learning

There are no mistakes. There is only learning. "How can that be?" you ask. Because "mistake" is judgment. We are simply choosing how we learn. We will all get there. When we get there is a matter of our choosing.

"I cannot choose your way. I can only choose My way. I can only choose MY way!"

"Where will it lead? Where I choose. I choose God. I choose to let go, no longer bound by that which held me for so long. No longer bound. I am free. Free to be me. Free to Be."

"Call Me. I know."

"Just, just, just...just what? Just what? Just Being. Just me."

God said, "Just come be...Just come be with Me."

"Hmm...uncertain is the way, uncertain is the path."

"No, not really if you trust. Trust in What is. Trust in Who is. You know. You know Who is. You know the Way, the Way back.

The Way to...you know. Just trust in the Way. You doubt. You question. I know. It is because you are afraid. It is okay. I can wait. I will be here. I am here. Just trust. Trust in the Way. Trust in yourself. Trust in Me. Yes, reach out your hand. I will have it and you. Umm hmm. Feels good doesn't it?"

"Yes."

"Still scared?"

"Yes."

"Yes, I know. Those first few steps, baby steps, but you are no baby. You have done this before. Yes, you have. It's okay, I promise. Yes, I promise it's okay. Still scared?"

"Yes."

"Okay. Rest. Breathe. Breathe. Breathe. See, less afraid, less fear. Your heart still beats fast. Just breathe. Just breathe. Come to Me. It's okay. Come to Me. Yes, baby steps. Remember? Yes, you remember. I see it in your smile. I see it in your eyes. Still scared? It's okay. Take your time. We have all of the time in the world. We have all of Eternity. Feel better?"

"Yes."

"Good. You don't have to get it right. You just have to get it. Get you. Get Me. It is alright."

"Thank You. Thank You for being the Father, my Father who art in Heaven, my Father who loves me, who comforts me. Thank

You. I get it. I feel it. Thank You. Thank You for love. Thank You for grace. Thank You for being me. Thank You for being everything."

"Thank you too for being My child, My wondrous creation. Home always welcomes you, is always open and available to you. Just come, come right in."

"It's good to be Home. Home again. Still feels a little scary. You are so big."

"But I am you."

"Yes, I know. I just don't know how I could be so big."

"But you are, My child—so big, so wondrous, so wonderful. I made you that way. How could it be otherwise?"

"I know, but that's what's so amazing. You are so big! I am so big! Life is so big! I'm just trying to take it all in, take You in. I want to get it—to get it all—to get You."

"You already have Me, have it all."

"But that's what so amazing, so awe...just leaves me in awe. How can I get all of this, take it in?"

"Just relax, just Be. It'll come, and the fear will subside. I promise because I am all there is, all that you know. Makes you smile and brings tears to your eyes."

"Yes, it's overwhelming."

"Yes, I know. Just breathe, just Be, just be with Me. Just go with Me."

"Okay. I'm breathing. Can You take my hand?"

"I can take your hand and all of you. I hold all of you close to Me all of the time. You are My child."

"Blessed be that I am Your child. I just want to be You."

"You are Me. You know this."

"Yes, I know, but it's scary. I get scared. You are so big, and I love You."

"Yes, I know and I love you. No one loves you more. You know this."

"Yes, I do. I'm trying to take it all in...all of You in me. It's all there. I can tell."

"Of course, it's all there. I'm all there in you. It couldn't be any other way. I made it that way, made it for you."

"Thank You, Father. Thank You for Your magnificence and grace. Thank You."

"You are welcome. It is yours. It has always been yours. It is yours at any time. It is yours all of the time. Heaven abounds in you. You are grace. You are Mine, and I am yours. That's how I made it. That's how it is. Now and Forever. Don't you see?"

"Yes, I see. You helped me to see. I am beginning to see through Your eyes. It is so magnificent, and I'm just seeing a glimmer!"

"It is you. It is you that you see. It is all made to be you."

"Me! What about everyone?"

"You and everyone, My Divine child."

"Thank You. You are indeed magnificent and everything! Such is the wonder of God! Thank You for opening my heart. Thank You for opening me. Thank You for being me. Thank You for being all that is. Thank You for being Heaven and Earth and the children's eyes. Thank You for spreading green life across the planet and for being the planet."

"It is Me and could be no other way. Now go to sleep, My child. We will speak again, and yes, you are getting it. You are awakening. Love to you always."

"Love to You too, my Father."

20

Broken Open

We are One with the Divine when we are Spirit. We "know" this because there is nothing else but Oneness. We come into the world with a spirit of innocence, reverence, joy, and love that is shaped by uplifting and wounding experiences. The world teaches us what it is to be human. We develop beliefs, behaviors, and habits as we interact with others. We believe we are our thoughts, our body, and our experiences. We believe our existence is limited to the perceptions of our five senses. We see the world and ourselves as flawed and limited.

This process causes us to gradually forget our Divinity as we journey into the body and the world. A veil descends separating us from the memory of our Divine Self, our Authentic Self, and all we seem to know is being human: the highs, the lows, the good, the bad, the pleasure, the pain, the beauty, the ugly, and the gruesome sometimes. We witness creativity followed by destruction. In some instances, life can be so traumatic that the veil morphs into an impenetrable fortress in an effort to protect ourselves from the world. Then we start to question, "Why am

I here? Is it just for this? Is this all there is?" This begins the journey back Home, back to our Authentic Self, back to the Divine.

We are broken open in order to unlearn what we know and remember what we have forgotten. We have to unlearn that we are of the world because we have forgotten our Divinity. Many of us require a breakdown in our lives in order to break through our beliefs and deeply entrenched habits to remember this. Breaking open allows for creating anew, for beginning again. It is a new space to reconnect to your True Self, your Divine Self. You were not meant to break. You were meant to rise like a new dawn upon the horizon—beautiful, luminous, awe-inspiring, and glorious! It is the Divine, and it is You! It's who you were always meant to be.

21

Lessons

As spiritual Beings, we come into the world to teach and to learn. All life experiences are an opportunity to learn lessons. The lesson is always there even in adversity. It's difficult to remember that in the midst sometimes, especially when those lessons are difficult or downright painful. Some days we feel like Oprah, "Jesus don't teach me nothing new today!"[11] But it's all just a learning opportunity. What they reveal to us is like the sun hidden behind the clouds—ever present and waiting to stream through and give light to our overcast existence. Nothing happening in our life is an accident or coincidence. It is Divinely ordered to assist our evolution. It's the lesson we need at that moment. So ask yourself, "What is this person or event here to teach me?" Know that whatever the answer is, you are being prepared for your ongoing journey. Remember this too as you "teach" others. When and how we learn life's lessons is our choosing.

22

Full Bloom

The flower blossomed, the petals opened, and I emerged. It was my True Self, the One the Divine had sent and always intended me to be. It was joy! It was grace! It was amazing to behold! The witnessing of God's intention come to fruition. There's no greater force than creation from the Master of all that is. See His intention made manifest as Life was blown in, and everything took shape. We took shape and were suddenly here amongst everything else, amongst all other life. How awesome to behold! He creates. We create and with the same vision, the same care, the same reverence because we understand our Oneness, wholeness, and responsibility to create like Him. How could it be otherwise when we are the same, are Him? There is peace and knowing certainty in this. There is no doubt because there is no separation. We know this just as we know where every star is in the heavens. We need but turn around, and there it is just as we knew it would be. We know our Self in the same way because we know Him with the same certainty. Can you come to this place? Will you take the journey? You need only extend your hand and take the steps. It is a walk of assuredness. There is no fear or doubt because you know this place. You have been here before. Oh, how your life will change in a way that's miraculous because you live with such knowing. Blink and it is done. Turn your head, and it is done. You are now living in the fullness of the Divine and in the fullness given to you by the Divine. This fullness enables you to create in a moment because there is not a shred of doubt or hesitancy, only knowingness that comes from being in complete alignment and unity with the Divine. There are no questions, only knowing. You just sit in the peace of God.

23

No Moment Is More
Important Than This One

No step is more important than the one you're on. No lesson is more important than the one in front of you. Not only is it important, but it is necessary. You cannot move forward until this moment is complete, until your learning is complete. Do not pass Go! Do not collect $200! You build one brick at a time. You advance one step at a time. You learn one lesson at a time. Joy comes when you embrace the moment and what occurs in the moment because you realize that this is what you needed. You didn't need, didn't benefit from what was missing. You needed what was right before you. It couldn't be otherwise. You are certain of this when you are aligned with the Divine because your knowingness is aligned with Universal Wisdom. It can all be revealed to you. Just ask. Just trust. Allow the magic of the Universe to reveal itself to you. See it all there before you. When you came from humanness, your awareness was too constricted to "see." But Being reveals the infinite and knows the rightness of everything. Can you step back and see it all in its proper place including you? I know you want to say, "No, not this," but yes, this too—all of it. It's all as it should be as you are all that you should be—infinite like the Universe—infinite like the Creator. Allow. Allow. Allow. Allow yourself to be One. Everything else already is.

24

Every Excess

Every excess is an attempt to assuage a broken heart. A piece of your heart was broken any time someone did something to you other than love you. The trauma evokes a pain that many seek to avoid by immersion in something or someone. Drugs, alcohol, gambling, and sex are well-known examples of addiction; however, we often seek comfort in many other excesses. These include eating, working, and shopping. Then there are the more subtle ones: the accumulation of money and power, perfectionism, hoarding, cleaning, plastic surgery, electronics, and relationships. We turn to temporary fixes over and over again instead of the real healing required by the pain in our hearts.

The pain of a broken heart is an aching hunger, an emptiness—a dark, lonely void—blindly driving us to seek comfort and fulfillment, but most importantly, relief. Please make the pain STOP! I can't bear anymore! It just won't go away. It feels bad. Sometimes it's so bad that I think I may die, and I don't want to die. I just want the pain to stop. Let me take this substance or do that activity to numb the pain so that it's bearable at least. Ahhhh! The pain subsides at least for a little while. I don't want to face it again. I will do many things, almost anything, to avoid feeling it again. I'll reach for these things over and over again to quell the ache.

There is a voice, small at first, which makes its way through to my consciousness, telling me that this is not the way. While I know this already, I cannot face the pain—cannot overcome it— and feel overwhelmed by it. It has become a frequent companion, one who is reluctant to leave. I'm not sure I'd know who I was without it, but I'd like to know. There has to be more than this. Surely, this isn't the reason I came here. Despite the dissonance, the voice seems to be growing in strength and volume. It is persistent and insistent. It seems to know me and is for me. Is it my champion? That is too much to hope for, but it continues to call to me. It tells me, "This is not the way. You are so much more, so much stronger than the pain whose grip you have succumbed to. It was a signpost, nothing more, but you've become ensnarled because you thought it was you."

You don't want to face your emotions and what drives you to make the choices that you do. You are afraid of what awaits you if you do. So you run and keep running as though your life depended upon it, but this only serves to get you farther and farther away from your Self. You run from one something to another: one relationship to another, one job to another, one house, one car, one income, one social status to another. Maybe you find momentary satisfaction or gratification, but you never find yourself in these things, this stuff. You continue to run, propelled by the fear that continues to hold you in its grip. Sometimes you aren't even aware that you are afraid, but if you feel worry, anger, regret, envy, impatience, superiority, inferiority, jealousy, frustration, or any negative emotion, these are expressions of fear.

At first, you only hear bits and pieces, then phrases, and then a string of sentences. What once seemed hopeless now has possibilities, but the pain will not surrender easily. While it's meant to be an indicator, its chronicity has it deeply entrenched and the cause buried far below the surface. Yet, the voice still calls to you: "This isn't who you are, and this isn't the way." At some point, you know you'll have to face the pain, and, more importantly, the cause; or live out a life of misery and could-have-beens. For some, the running never stops until their last breath passes. This is their lot because they will not face the pain or demons they fear lying in wait—the ones that wrought the pain in the first place.

There are others, who will heed the call to recognize their Self. It may be early in the journey, or it may be when they can run no longer—lying spent and exhausted—only to realize that they could not get away from themselves no matter how far or fast they went. It's hard to see a way out, but you peel it back one layer at a time. It is laborious and painstaking work. Sometimes only inches are revealed during the excavation, and sometimes you stop because it's just too much to bear. Inevitably, you pick it back up and continue the work. The voice continues to be a source of encouragement and is a sharp reminder when you would regress. Then one day the light streams through as you uncover the source of your pain and its little minions. Yes, your heart aches. It's a sadness you didn't want to face but knew that you must so that it could pass like so much floating debris, and your healing could begin.

The pain is a call to return Home. We fail to recognize this, and try to medicate it like a headache with a pain reliever. The pain is a guide to discovering that you are far more than you think you are. You are far more than you believed yourself to be. You've spent your whole life running from your True Self, and in doing so, running from the fullness of the Divine. Will you accept the invitation to explore who you are? Are you willing to trust in the Way, to trust in your Self, to trust in the One? Are you willing to sit with the pain as a doorway into who you are instead of who you are not? "How do I do that?" you ask. Ask yourself, "What am I feeling? What event and thoughts led to the feeling? Am I the event or feeling?" If the answer is "No," then be still without reaching for something to relieve the pain. If you do this, you will find that the pain will subside eventually. Initially, this may be quite difficult, and you may reach for something to ease your discomfort. Be compassionate with yourself, and do not judge. It will get easier with each attempt.

Once the pain passes without anything to numb it, a space is left. You can sense a presence when your attention is focused on this space. Who is this presence? It is You, the Divine You. This presence and space is akin to sitting on a river bank watching the water flow by. You are the Observer. The pain, events, and thoughts are the river. Your arrival to this space means you are now Home! Home is You, also known as the Observer or Divine Consciousness. The revelation is that it was your Divine Self you were seeking all along. This is where fullness resides. It is always within. It's like taking a journey across the world seeking a great treasure only to return home and realize that the treasure was at home within you the whole time. So it is okay to stop seeking your happiness, joy, and fulfillment in others and in things. It's okay to let go! You don't have to fear never finding it or losing it as everything outside of you changes and evolves because you have always had these expressions of your Divinity within you. You were always Divine because it was a gift and your birthright from the Creator of all that is.

The Divine gave us to the world with a heart filled with Him and filled with love, but the world taught us to fear. Every decision you make is based upon love or fear. Live Life from a place of love! Happiness, joy, compassion, gratitude, creativity, and reverence are manifestations of love. They enrich and uplift us. It'll take time for many of us, but that's okay because you are doing the work that we are all called to do. Now, you can be the Divine's intended gift to the world. This is the fullness granted to you by the One.

25

Gifts

A gift is truly given when the recipient is in a place to receive it. Otherwise, it's as though it was never given at all. Are you open to receiving and honoring the gifts given to you by others and the Divine—including this day?

26

Tell Me of the Soul...

The Soul is immortal. It is...eternal; like the winds of time, like the perpetual dawning of every new day, like stillness and Forever after. It is a pulse that always beats and a story that never ends. The Soul is, even when stars cease shining and universes collide. It is the eternal bloom of the Universe...Life expressed. Who could imagine this? Only the Creator of all that is...God is Life.

The Soul is the essence of our very existence. It is always there for us to turn to when we grow weary of our plight. It waits patiently, knowing that we shall return one day, and why not? It has all of eternity and is Eternity stretched out before us. It is the path. It is the Way. It leads us back Home when we have lost our way. It is comfort. It is shelter. It is reassurance. If you do not know, just ask; and revealed to yourself you will be. Unexpected this is. Wow! I am happiest here and need nothing more. Besides, what is beyond infinity? Just clarity. Inward is where I dwell.

The Soul is the source of creativity and imagination. It is Being. Who would we *be* without it? We would not. We could not. Only a shell would we be without it. It calls to us. It guides us with the wisdom of the Universe, of all that Is. Where would we be without it? Who knows? Who, where, how would—no. That would mean No One, and there is One. There is no Soul without One. How does One describe the Soul? One does not. It just is because it was created to be everything. Everything for me. Everything for you. Everything within us all of the time. Can you grasp this? Do you get this? I know it's like knowing Eternity, but that is the point—to know Eternity all of the time.

Nothing, "No thing," else really matters. You've been here before but have forgotten. It's okay because you will remember again, can't help but to know again, eventually. When is up to you—whenever you decide to awaken. Then you will "see" everything—will know everything. Then No Thing else will matter. This is joy! This is peace! This is freedom! Can you imagine anything so wondrous? Come join me. Come join your Soul. It awaits you along with all of the others that constitute the One. It is all One. You are all One. Remember your knowing. Remember your Self. Return to your Self. You already know.

27

Life Calls

Your life calls to you. It's a yearning that urges you to be the miracle you were destined to be when you first drew breath, and it urges you to be a living life's work that's in service to others as well as yourself. There are gifts to the world within you that can only be manifested through You. Your unwillingness to answer the call means dying inside. It's existing. It's surviving, but it's not living in fullness. Will you awaken from your slumber? Will you heed the call from your Soul to be that singular light, giving warmth and illumination to the world in a way that only you can?

28

Looking for the Divine

Many search for the Divine for a long time and over many miles. You do not need to find the Divine because He is not lost! Besides, He is You! He is everyone and everything! So He is in you and before you all of the time. Your charge is to be Him and to manifest Him in every moment. So stop looking, and Be!

29

Sadness

(Crying)
"Who Being?
How Being?
What is my Being?
What would it be?
Well Being...all is well with my Being."

"Why the sadness then?"

"That comes from a different place, a different space. Being reassures this other. All is well...All is well with my Soul." (Smiling)

"See, I told you so. You just have to let go of what you hoped for, and allow what needs to come forth to *be* in existence. I know you had your heart set on the other. It is okay. I promise. It'll be so much better."

"Promise?"

"I promise. I know it hurts. I know you hurt. There's been so much disappointment, and you've tried so hard. Nothing seems to work, but that is not so little One. I see you. I see your tears. It's all okay. I promise."

"Promise?"

"Yes. Just come to Me. Remember I always love you. You can always be with Me. I'll always love you. Your tears seemed to have slowed. Your heartache seems less. I know you are unsure, but if you'll allow things to unfold, you'll be surprised."

"Who is it?"

"I know that you like to know, but that would ruin the surprise! Just come sit with Me. Just come be in My comfort. I will hold you close for now."

"What about for always?"

"What about for always? You already know about for always. I just want you to *be* here for now. Always will come. It can't help but come. Comfort right now is what you need. So come be with Me now. "

"Okay." (Sigh)

"Always so hesitant you are, but it's okay. See, isn't that better?"

"Yes, somewhat."

"Yes, I know. It takes time, and time is all we have. We have all of the time in the world. See, it's starting to ease."

"Yes, I feel a little better. Thank You. Will I ever get this right?"

"Yes, some day and that's okay—whenever it is."

"Are You sure?"

(Smiles) "Of course, you would ask that question when what you really mean is, 'Am I sure?' You know that it is you that's uncertain. This too will pass some time."

"I feel tired. I want to go to sleep."

"I know. I wanted you to feel comforted. I wanted you to rest well and easily, but I still feel your sadness."

"Will You hold me?"

"All of the time."

(Smiling) "I just want to feel comforted. I want the sadness to go away."

"It will. Do not worry. It will pass as sure as that beautiful smile lights up your face. You know I gave that to you."

(Smiling)

"See, there you go again. That's what I like to see. Remember, I can be your everything. You just have to allow Me to be."

"I know. Will You hold me while I go to sleep? I'm working on getting there. I have it some moments but lose it in others."

"I know. It's okay. You'll get there. In the meantime, you always have Me."

"Thank God! I mean Thank You! That gives me some comfort. I mean some of the sadness is still there."

"I know what you meant. It's okay. When you learn to fully trust Me, this will pass. It will all go away like a bad dream. I promise. Give me your hand."

"Okay."

"Now, give me your heart."

"Okay."

"You did that with little hesitation. You did good."

"It's because I love You."

"I know you do. I love you too."

"I just want to do Your will."

"I know that too. I know. It's time for you to go to sleep. I will hold you so you can rest easily."

"Thank You, Father."

"You are always welcome, and I am always here. Sweet dreams, My child; and yes, you are always My child."

"Into Eternity?"

"Yes, into Eternity. I promise. Now close your eyes, and go to sleep."

"Yes, Father."

30

Fear Was My Companion

Little did I know, but fear was my constant companion. It clung to me like a dark, heavy hooded cloak. I thought it provided protection, and in some ways, it did. It kept me from revisiting some dark, isolated places; but in other ways, it drove me to flee like a beast being whipped by its master to run faster and faster. There were also times when it flew up at my throat and threatened to rip away my last vestiges of valor! It had me in its grip, and I thrashed about—desperately trying to free myself. I would manage to be free for a brief time, only to find myself back in its sinister clutches once again. Would I ever be able to free myself once and for all? It was clear that I would have to because no one else would.

The haunting moans of many other captives echoed all around me as evidence of those whose fates were sealed by an escape that proved elusive. You could see the pain of their capture on their narrow, hollowed out faces and sunken eyes that conveyed resignation to their fate. I knew that I would stand alongside them—resigned as they were—if I gave up; but my heart would have none of this! It knew that I had a destiny, and it was not this!

It would not surrender to this misery, but knew it and I must surrender to He who called me.

So despite repeated efforts by fear to drag me back and suck me into its vortex, I was determined to claw my way out. I knew the voice of the One who called to me, and I would not, could not be turned away even by myself. Ultimately, it is us who succumbs to our personal demons when we would blame others just as it is us who chooses to ascend beyond our meager beliefs about ourselves. I would not be turned away from what I instinctively knew was there waiting for me. It was my future, but more importantly, it was me, so much bigger than the little meager me I imagined myself to be. It was there waiting for me if I would just grab hold, and I was determined to do just that. There were many times when I surpassed what others believed about me, and I was determined to surpass what I feared about myself.

The Divine was calling to me, and I was calling to myself because reaching forward was all that I could do. Remaining mired in a morass of fear and disbelief was akin to a living death, and Life was trumpeting loudly! It was a sound I could not resist because it meant a future that I sensed was grand and unimaginable in its scope and magnitude.

* * * * * * * * * * * * *

I began meditating on abundance—in this case, aligning consistently with the Divine. I feared answering His call meant becoming God-intoxicated, which would cause the desire for a mate to evaporate. Then the stream of God Consciousness began.

He said, "Come go with Me. Do you know who you are? You are Mine. You worry about what you will have to give up. There is nothing to give up. You have so much to gain. You don't even know. You have no idea. There is so much—"

"Abundance?"

"—abundance waiting for you with Me through Me. So you see there is nothing to give up except your misery, your fear, your inadequacy. There is richness and fullness here with Me. You call it the Land of Milk and Honey. I call it Forever. Yes, that's right, Forever. Remember? I see that you do. It's familiar. It's comforting. It's You."

"Me?"

"That's right. It's You because You too are everything. You are a part of the Oneness of everything. I tell it to you in a way that I hope you will understand. Yes, I know it's redundant, but I hope you will understand."

My son climbed into bed with me. He's such a challenge.

"Yes, that baby is a blessing, as challenging as he may be. I want you to get, no, trust in the Oneness of everything because then you will understand, will know, that you don't have to go without. It's all there for you. Let go. It may not show up how you want, but it will show up. You will not go without. It will be better and more than you expected."

"Promise?"

"I promise."

"Thank You."

"You are welcome, My child."

"I want to go to sleep."

"Okay then. Go to sleep. I told you this because you were excited, and I knew that you couldn't sleep."

"Yes, I know. I'm excited because You are absolutely amazing! The way You give wisdom to me and allow me to express it in such a creative way. It's just amazing! It makes it hard to sleep."

"I'm glad to see you so excited and happy, but sleep now."

"Okay, but I'll need Your help. I'm too excited!"

"It's okay. I promise there will be more."

"I know, but I don't know if I can take it! It's just amazing... the magic of the Universe that is You. Good God!"

"You are sweet. It's nice to see you so excited. Now sleep."

"Okay, Father. I'll try, but help."

"Okay. Done."

I closed my eyes after lying on my pillow.

"I'm back!"

"I know."

"I'm too excited to sleep!"

"I know that too."

"I love talking to You and being with You!"

"You are with Me always, and I am with You always."

"Is it that simple?"

"Yes, it's that simple. Wherever You are, there too will You find Me."

"That's easy. I keep forgetting."

"You don't really forget. You disconnect, and that's when you struggle. Now, you are reconnected, and You know. There is no struggle. You just flow. So you must be connected all of the time. Remember Eternity?"

"Yes, I remember Eternity. Be and know Eternity all of the time." (Smiling)

"Yes, that's it! That's *being* and knowing Me all of the time. Ready to sleep?"

"I believe so. I think so."

"Okay. Now rest."

"Yes, Father."

31

My Warrior King

Valiant
Fierce
Wise
Honorable
Inspiring
Extraordinary
The Soul of you calls out to me.
You would have my loyalty.
You would have me.
You call to me across the miles.
You call to me across our lives.
My heart is yours just as your heart is mine.
This we know throughout time.
So seek.
So search.
So find.
The love you seek is forever thine.
So come home to rest no longer weary.
To the comfort of my arms that long to hold you dearly.

32

Love Is...

It is the nature of being human to seek ourselves in others. That's what we call being in love. It's the recognition of our self in the other. The more we see our self in the other, the more we love them. We see our highest self, both what we are and what we could be, in our beloved. We hope the other will give to us what we believe we are missing, failing to realize that we already have those qualities and that person within. It can be difficult to recognize this because it can buried under many layers of living, but you already are and have within you all that you aspire to *be*. The blessing in being well loved by the other is that they become the conduit through which you discover this. Their love becomes a mirror that allows you to see yourself in novel and remarkable ways. All that you wish to hold is already within your heart. You are your Darling. You are your Beloved. You are Love.

33

Come to Me

Come to Me.
Of course, I would come to Thee.
I would happily sit at Your feet.
It's a place of joy!
It's the place to *be*.
Is there any other?
It's a place of wonder!
Many know it.
Others still seek it.
When you find it, you won't want to leave it.
Surely this is where I was meant to *be*.
This is where I am free.
This is where I bloomed,
And became what God intended for me.
Flowing and Graceful
Magnificent and Beautiful
Who imagined anything so lovely?
God did,
Over and over,
And He will again,
Bolder and bolder.
He sees in ways that are beyond complex.
He saw us, and we drew breath.

So again I will come,
Or I will go.
I will do His will,
Or *be* His will.
I will flow.

34

Radiate Love, Light, and Life

Let your living be an expression of the love, light, and Life given to you when you first twinkled in your momma's belly. It was given wings and took flight when you first drew breath. Allow it to fill you and radiate from You every day such that your light is evident and the abundance of it blankets and uplifts those You encounter on every part of your journey. Doing this allows You to reach past the distressed appearance of another's personhood to illuminate the Soul of who *they* are. This, You see in them even if they do not see it in themselves. You give them light even if it is only for a brief time. For some, it is this warmth, comfort, and the promise of a better tomorrow that enables them to stay here beyond today. So do not underestimate the brilliance within You and its transformative possibilities for others! You can make the day brighter and magnificent along with the lives You have touched during your time here.

35

Two Joined Souls

It is a love that nurtures, nourishes, enriches, and transforms. It transcends the physical and what is human because it is of the Spirit. It is an expression of the energy generated by two connected Souls. It flows freely and easily. Yes, there is delicious passion, but there is always an underlying tenderness to their way with each other. It is fed and sustained by the energy of love that each gives to the other in service to the other. It calms both, and nothing about it feels like work. It is done because One knows that this is what is necessary to benefit the other at this time. They each know this about the other because they allow the other to know. They recognize each other as a precious gift and happily treasure each other like sparkling gems. This is grounded in honesty, integrity, and regard for the well-being of the other that equals their own. They understand that harming the other means harming themselves. Their ultimate wish is to create a union worthy of exaltation! It is their hearts speaking to each other. It is the magic of two joined Souls.

36

Dragon Slayer

"We must be willing to get rid of the life that we've planned so as to have the life that is waiting for us."

~ Joseph Campbell

We are human beings, not human doings. Much of our time is spent doing, but there is that special something that you could happily do all day. What do you love to do? So much so that time just seems to fly away. You feel happy, excited, energized, and joyful! The energy of it and you flow freely and easily, giving light to those around you. This is your bliss. This is your calling. This is your gift. It comes from your Divine Self or Being. If you could shed your fears, doubts, others' expectations, and societal values, you would happily do this every day. Many times we get caught up in concerns like, "Will I make a lot of money? What will others think? Will I be successful? I should do something else. I don't know how to do this, and I'm scared!"

First of all, do not SHOULD upon yourself! The expectations for your life, whether from you or others, are relevant only if they are aligned with your life's calling, if they serve others as you fulfill that calling, and if your Spirit guides you in this way. Otherwise, SHOULD is someone else's dream for you and your uncertainty for yourself.

Second, it's okay to be afraid and uninformed because your Being knows your gift and purpose. It already knows what to do. If you step back and allow it to guide you, your Spirit will impart this knowledge to you; and your gift will flow like water. So hold your fears close and reassure them and you that your Divine Self will shepherd you safely through.

Third, you can't help but be successful when you are directed by Being. This success means you have been in service to others. It may or may not mean financial prosperity, but you will have enough. It also doesn't mean there won't be struggle, but are you willing to do what's required so that you can excel at what you love? There's always room for excellence, and prosperity often follows. Pursue what you love to do, and let prosperity chase you.

Finally, courage means doing what you must even though you are afraid. There is security in choosing the well-trodden path, but if it isn't what you love, you'll also find drudgery, boredom, and suffocation there. There will be a nagging emptiness and regrets about what your life could have been had you been courageous enough to follow your heart and manifest your gifts. It's uncertain how many heroes there are amongst us, but will you be the hero in your life and slay your own dragons?

37

Happy New Year!

May you have the eyes to "see" the Divinity in people and "know" the perfection inherent in the rhythm of Life. Also, "know" that what we all want is to be loved, affirmed, and accepted for who we are at any given moment in spite of our behavior or choices. Are you willing to reach past the challenges of how others behave because you can "see" the perfect Divine Being created by the One? Do you "know" that we all manifest perfection when our consciousness is ready? May the New Year be a gift to you, and may you be a gift of Life-affirming Love to others.

38

Swirled

It was an orange sky,
Streaked with gold,
Swirled with reds, purples, and gray.
It was the Heavens,
Sought here on Earth.
Can you see yourself?
Maybe.
What I see are chances,
Chances in a life gone by,
Chances yet to come.
All swirled together
Like a candy cane.
All swirled together
Like a hurricane.
What could I do?
I don't know.
What shall I do?
That remains to be seen.

I see the face of God.
Here I shall stay.
Forever is not long enough.
Swirling,

Glowing,
Streaking,
Holding,
Holding my breath
At the immenseness of it all.
Nothing else matters,
But that can't be too.
It is the Universe,
Grand and small,
Meaningful and irrelevant.
It is all and nothing,
Swirled into a ball.
Can you see?
Can you feel?
Do you know?
Knowing is all there is,
Swirled into a ball.

Reds, purples, grays, and blues
In all of its many hues.
It is the color of Life.
It is the color of Love.
It is the color of You.
Can You sit with God?
Can You sit in stillness?
Can You just *be* here?
And not wish to *be* elsewhere.
There really is nowhere else to *be* anyway.
You always come back to You,
Even when you do not wish to.
You only appear to have left,
And all You want to do is return.
Your Self calls you to return.
The Divine says, "Come be with Me."

It is an invitation to *be* with You.
I know you feel it.
You feel Him and all that Is.
"Just come be with Me."
It's as simple as "Okay."

39

I Give to You

I give to you
Because it was given to me.
I give to you
Because it is what you needed.
In times of plenty,
In times of few,
It is there to be given unto you.
I give to you in regard of you,
In reverence of you.
It is our Divinity speaking to each other.
It is there with you all of the time.
Can you feel it?
Ever so close,
Ever so free flowing,
It is the rhythm of your heart.
It is the beat of the Serengeti.
Oneness giving to the One,
Oneness giving to Itself.
It is joy!
It is a peace of the ages.
Thump, thump
It beats within.

All that you need is within you to give.
I am just here to show you.
You are here to know this and more.
Feel it within your Soul.
Feel it within your very Being.
It speaks to you.
It whispers to you to remember You.
This is the true Gift,
Giving You back to you
In its vastness, depths, and splendor.
And so the circle begins again,
Forever in motion,
Forever a notion,
Nevermore, and
Forevermore
Once again.

Will it stop?
It cannot.
It is a cycle,
That seeks to express itself in something new.
So it cannot.
Just go with it,
Knowing that You are Forever
And Forever never stops.
You are perpetuity.
Just as your giving is perpetual,
From a wellspring.
Rest easily in that you have much to give.
Your Spirit is always full,
And never runs dry.
It is eternal and Eternity,
And so too are You and I.

40

Yearning

I yearn for you,
Forgetting you are always with me.
I sense your presence when I am still,
Through a connection Divine.
It speaks to me without language.
It speaks with knowing.
It is all there.
Nothing else is needed,
So rest easily.
"I hold you close all of the time."
It was God speaking.
It was God *being*.
I thought it was about someone else.
It was,
But it was Him as someone else.
It always brings us back to Him.

41

Masterpiece

Many of us live our lives as a side bar, a side note, an afterthought. It's something we get around to after everything else is done and after everyone else has been cared for. This is the most short-sighted kind of presumptuousness. We keep believing that there will always be water in the well to draw despite our failure and sometimes unwillingness to nourish or replenish ourselves. Is it any wonder that we are exhausted and running on empty? We, like many other living beings, require many of the same life-sustaining essentials. These include sleep, nutritious food, shelter, safety, community, and for human beings, a sense of their place in the universe.

Women in particular want to make others the center of their existence. Women give to and care for others because it is their nature to do so but also in the hope that others will give them what they need so that they can be fulfilled. Welcome to Fantasy Island! At some point, reality sets in, oftentimes after many decades of seeking fulfillment in others, who neither could nor wanted to meet our idealized, unrealistic expectations. Prince

Charming is broken down on the side of the road, and the cavalry isn't coming to save you either!

While experiences and relationships are central, they are not your center. Only you can be that for yourself. It is ourselves that we need to turn to, that we need to ask, "What do you need? How can I fulfill you?" After you board an airplane and before takeoff, the flight attendant says, "Should the cabin lose pressure, oxygen masks will drop from overhead…If you are traveling with a small child…secure your mask first then assist them." The point, of course, is that you may pass out and be unavailable to help your child if you fail to put your mask on prior to assisting them. So it's not only about your survival but about the survival of those you care about. You must care for and strengthen yourself in order to be available for others. Iyanla Vanzant says, "Fill your own cup first then give from your overflow." In other words, keep yourself full and give the extra, the "overflow," to others.

When you fail to fill yourself, you have less and less to give until nothing is left for anyone including yourself. The well ran dry! Some may say this is selfish, but what is really selfish and unfair is to expect others to be what we need in order to have our needs met. Disappointment is inevitable when we rely upon others to nourish us. We feel bereft and resentful because they cannot or will not. People give us what they want, when they want, and if they want. The reality is that no one can meet all of our needs. That is our responsibility. If you were in good health and had money to feed yourself, would you wait for someone else to do it? For a short time, possibly. Now, under the same circumstances, would you allow your hunger to progress to starvation? Absolutely not! It's as important to nourish the empty spaces of your life just as you would your physical hunger. Neale Donald Walsch said, "If you do not go within, you go without."[12] You cannot expect the world to love you, to cherish you, to value you more than you are willing to give that to yourself.

Look to you—that amazing, creative, miraculous you—for the fertile seeds of your magnificent life! Can you see yourself as the artist, the creator, and cultivator of your life? Imagine you are a sculptor. What material and tools would you need? What type of space and lighting? How would you shape and mold the raw material? What happens when your creation takes shape in unexpected ways? What if you have to start over? Despite the struggle, turmoil, and doubt, you still feel the call of the creative process. Be patient and compassionate with yourself through the setbacks. Yes, there will be setbacks, but it's the journey that matters. You watch your vision unfold as you start anew. You are persistent and persevere because you know there is a masterpiece within you. You marvel at it when it is done because even you did not imagine anything so grand, but wait! What is that at the center? The only true center—you!

Make you the center of your masterpiece! "How do I do that?" you ask. You must nourish your Divinity and connection to the Divine. This is where your joy, fulfillment, and peace reside. All of your questions can be answered by your Divine Self. So ask, "What steps do I take? What would it take to make me delicious?" Yes, feel the smile that lights up your face and the mischievous, somewhat forbidden delight that wells up inside of you at the thought of being delicious. Is it nurturing, sleep, exercise, adventure, stillness, or clarity? Whatever it is, give it to yourself in abundance! Fill yourself with love, compassion, and laughter! Then you have that to give to others. Celebrate your life in every moment! Knowing that you have the ability to nourish yourself gives you ease because you now understand that you will never have to go without. You no longer look outside of yourself and can give to yourself abundantly You have set yourself free to create a life that's engaged, meaningful, and limitless. It's a life well lived. It's a life filled with precious discoveries including the most precious one of all—you!

42

Victory

We achieve our greatest victory by facing and then overcoming our greatest fear. We journeyed along a path that ultimately led us to face ourselves. There were no more dark places to scurry off to, no more places to hide. Facing ourselves allowed us to embrace ourselves in all of our many facets including our jagged edges. These served us too by bringing us this far and developing us until we became rounded and smoothed like jewels of the Nile. The Divine imbued us with unlimited, boundless possibilities! We were liberated by facing then embracing all that we are, including those parts that chose to hide in the shadows. We are free to live life as the brilliant, fiery, luminous Beings that the Divine created by facing what cast the longest shadow during the darkest night.

43

Realization

I realized that each time my heart beat
That was the Divine loving me.
I realized that every step I took was a prayer,
A prayer that asked that I allow myself to *be*,
All that was asked of me.
Every movement was a meditation,
Every thought a celebration,
Every breath an exaltation
Of the Life force within me,
Moving and mingling with those about me.
I am God's masterpiece in motion.
To Him, air in devotion,
His prayer come to Life.
There was a lot of love in that prayer.
There was a lot of love in me.
I see Him looking upon us
With loving eyes,
Smiling at His creations,
Patient with us too,
Knowing that at some point
We will look to Him,
After realizing it was all there
The bounty spread before us

So easy to see
If only One has the eyes
If only One will *be*
All that He dreamed,
All that He conceived,
All that He believed,
The Love,
The Light,
Just exquisite
In flight,
In Him, my Liege.

44

So Grateful!

Oh, the joy of sitting in stillness.
I feel the beat of my heart.
I feel the flow of my breath,
And the Life force coursing through my body,
Because of the two.
I am so grateful!
So grateful for this!
So grateful for having a moment,
To experience the simplicity of it all,
And the magnitude of it all.
I am so grateful for Life!
So grateful for my loved Ones,
That have shepherded me to this point.
So grateful for the consciousness,
That allows me to soak it all in like the warm rays of the sun.
My heart speaking to the heart of another
Is an amazing, unforgettable experience.
Feeling their energy shift to a place of ease
Because their heart has been spoken to
Gives me grace.
It is gratifying and makes me smile.

45

Pulled Forward

Get a vision! Iyanla Vanzant said, "A vision will pull you forward."[13] Intention and attention are two components of the process. Having a vision means that you intend to create a specific outcome or manifestation. You are transforming what is into something else new and different. This is transformation. In order for your vision or transformation to occur, it requires energy also known as your attention. Focusing your energy on your vision feeds it and makes it grow. Otherwise, it's an idea, like many, that languish and wither on the vine.

Your vision vibrates at a certain frequency, and as you expand your vision by adding details and giving it shape, your vision will feed you by giving you energy. You are excited and work enthusiastically! Enthusiasm means, "In God." Your vision moves to a higher frequency, which is associated with the positive emotions you are feeling. So, you see, you nourish your vision, and your vision nourishes you. It's a circular process. Your connection to your vision causes your frequency to change to a higher value as well. Your thoughts and actions will change to this new frequency in order to accommodate this shift and transformation of you and your vision. In essence, your vision pulls you forward by changing your frequency to match its own. You are drawn to your ever-expanding vision, and both of you assist each other in your advancement.

For example, you envision building a home. You imagine what the land looks like and where your home will rest. You envision the type of architecture, the number of bedrooms and bathrooms, the size of the kitchen, the types of cabinets, flooring, lighting, paint colors, furnishings, etc. As it takes shape, you can feel what it will be like to live in it and are excited by the prospect. You work fervently to finish. Your home is finally built, and what was a vision intended by you is now a reality because you were focused on it, giving it energy. As it transformed, you became excited and buoyed by your creation, which gave you energy in return. And so, the cycle continued—the creator giving to its creation and vice versa. They each pulled the other forward until the unmanifest became manifest.

This, too, is the process of the Universe. The Creator gives to its Creation, and the Creation gives to the Creator. In doing so, the Creation becomes the Creator. The Creator decides to create and allows its Universal Wisdom to organize the details trusting that it will do so magnificently! It never worries. The Creator just trusts. The Creator just creates, and It creates spectacularly!

46

Rhythm

When you've done your best and Life follows a different path, let go. Don't hold Life, insisting that It *be* a certain something when It needs to *be* something else. Let It be. Let It *be* as It is because It is that already. It will still go where It will, slipping through your grasp. The question is whether you will suffer outside of It or flow with It. Learn to PAUSE and listen to the rhythm of Life. It beats as surely as your own heart does. It will always guide you if you listen to Its rhythm, ask "Now what?" and then listen again for Its answer.

47

Sensuous Kiss

Soft,
Slow,
Sensuous,
One to be savored.
It is the promise of something more.
Our breathing becomes labored.
It is tender in its exploration,
A sweet succulence not to be missed.
And who would want to,
Who would want to resist?
Carefully exploring the secrets within.
Tasting them one at a time.
Then back again.
Tasting lips,
Then the soft insides;
A choreographed dance,
As the two collide.
Dipping,
Slipping,
Holding me close.
Guiding us to the abyss.
Hoping it is all that it promises.
Heartbeats quicken.

Pulses pound.
Swaying to and fro.
Then come the sounds.
Sounds of pleasure slip from our lips.
Then tingling starts in the groin and hips.
A throbbing ache begging to be unleashed;
All of this ignited by a
Soft,
Slow,
Sensuous kiss.

48

Grab Hold!

When you trust that God is Life, and when you trust that you are wonderful, amazing, awesome, beautiful, and powerfully creative, you will experience the magic and beauty of the Universe. You will know that Life has always been right there for you, waiting for you to grab hold! You will know that your connection with others can extend beyond what you see in front of you, and you will connect with them on a Soul-to-Soul level. So grab hold of Life, and experience the magic and majesty that is You!

49

Feeding

"Quit feeding that weed!"

~ Josephine Hood

We bring energy to every moment of our existence. When we're running low, we may attempt to feed on the energy of another. This may satisfy us for a while, but the effect wanes, their energy runs low, or they may attempt to feed off of us! Then you've got two hungry people trying to feed off of each other. What a mess! Given the intention of the creators, is it any wonder that this was the manifestation?

We all have areas of our lives that aren't in alignment with who we are and no longer serve us. When you "quit feeding that weed," it no longer has energy or nourishment to sustain itself and passes away. Do not give your time, energy, thoughts, or emotions to situations or people in your life that you would sooner see gone. Allow them to pass as you would a breeze. Gone as suddenly as they came and a memory just as quickly.

Be conscious of your intentions as you interact with others. Be mindful of the energy you bring and the energy brought to you. Is it uplifting and inspiring, or draining and disheartening? Are folks happy to see you coming, or are they going the other way? Allow others to bring to you only that which nurtures and strengthens you. Be a gift that enriches the heart of others and stirs their imagination.

50

Idol

Idol worshipping is the seeking of your joy, happiness, and peace outside of the Divine, your Spirit, and the spiritual union between the two. You have put your hopes and faith in something temporary instead of placing it in That which is eternal and Eternity. Choose Infinity! It always awaits you and never disappoints you. It sustains you, never leaving you without. It is a concerto—beautifully written, beautifully played. It invites you to be with your Self. It invites you to be the One.

51

Divine, Take the Wheel!

The rejection of Life, in whatever form it is expressed in any moment, is a rejection of the Divine Source of the Universe and Its impeccable wisdom. Acceptance is the acknowledgment of the existence of something or someone as it is in that moment. You have not sanctioned an occurrence by accepting it. You have only acknowledged it and the fact that it can't be changed once it occurs. Accepting what occurs in the moment means accepting the Divine, His wisdom, and aligning with Him. Now that you are aligned with Him, the actions You take are directed by Spirit and serve all Life.

52

No Emptiness

You are the Divine's expression to the world. There is no emptiness in that. There is only the fullness granted to You from the very beginning. You have come here to *be* a light and to cast away darkness wherever You find it as only You can. You have the ability to transform this moment, this day, and eternity by *being* His intended gift to the world. Your magnificence casts a brilliance that is difficult to look upon but draws many who seek to bask in its healing warmth. Others see it in You. Others feel it in You. Now is the time for you to embrace it within Your Self! Be His gift! Be light!

53

Ooo Wee!

Smoldering eyes with passion
Always ready to ignite
Exploring my body in ecstasy
Taking me higher and higher
Climbing new heights
Your hands played my body like a Stradivarius
Leaving me luminous until nothing was left
Except for the sweetness between us
And the desire to linger
Holding each other close
Until again things turned steamier
This was love in a myriad of forms
Exciting and scintillating
Joyful and titillating
Breathless and undulating
We can't let go
Not now
Not for a lifetime
Not even then
Nothing and no one could ever be this good
At least not until the next time
Upon the pinnacle we stood
Wrapped within each other

Leaping from the precipice
Landing gently, softly
Making sure nothing was missed
As we would do this over and over
Oh, the sweetness of this
Come close, please closer
So that I may lay my head upon your chest
Drifting off to sleep
Dreamily remembering us
Listening to your heartbeat
Rest for now is what we need
Until we begin once again
The delicious making of Ooo Wee!

54

Secret Dream

Comedian, author, and talk show host Chelsea Handler said her secret dream is to "end up with a guy who loves and adores me. He would think the world of me and would move mountains for me. It would be a big love story, a beautiful love story."[14] Don't many of us want that? It occurred to me that I already have that in the Divine. He loves and adores me and moves mountains for me even when those mountains are in my own heart or head. Guess what? He loves and adores you in the same splendid way! There's no mountain high, wide, or deep enough that He can't move. He always loves you, and He's always with you. There's no bigger or more beautiful love story than the one you have with the Divine.

55

You Are My Joy!

Father, You are my joy!
You are my heart.
You are my heartbeat.
You are my everything.
You are my smile.
You are That which makes me sing!
Oh, to be taken over,
To be taken to the place.
I couldn't imagine this.
See the sun shine.
It is heavenly bright.
See the evidence.
You come to Be here in us.
Take me where You want me to go.
I will follow.
This I promise.
I will get there.
This You already know;
Even though others may not.
Rise up to be what You called.
Rise up to be.
My heart rests easily,
In Your grace,

In Your comfort,
In all That is You,
In all That is me.

I Am Your world.
I Am the world.
I Am so much more;
Even to those who do not know.
Rest easily.
I see.
I know.
I know Everything.
I know You.
You are Everything.
There is no other,
Only You as the other,
Only You as Everything.
Hasten to You.
Hasten to Home.
I am here now.
I am at peace and with You,
Knowing the Divine order,
Knowing You.
Thank You for lifting the veil.
Thank You for sharing Your tale,
Of the giftedness of us all.
I remain,
Your humble servant.

56

Details, Details, Details!

Commit to a vision then expect what you need to show up! Many of us do the exact opposite when it comes to life. We have a hope, a dream, a calling, and we don't move forward because we don't have everything we need to make it happen. We aren't the right age. We don't have the money, the time, or the right opportunity, background, or location. We just don't! Instead, commit to creating your heart's desire, and trust the Divine to work it out. Trust His Divine Wisdom to organize the details. I promise you that He will because this is the same Divine Consciousness that created the Universe, its trillions of planets and stars, and you, who are made of star dust.

Dr. Simon Haley, the father of *Roots* author Alex Haley, worked as a train porter to earn money for college. He met a man on the train one day and shared his desire to get his degree. Simon didn't have enough money and didn't know how he would get it either. The young Mr. Haley also told the gentlemen the name of the college he hoped to attend. Unbeknownst to Simon, the gentleman contacted the college and paid his tuition with the instruction that Simon be told ONLY if he showed up. This was a test of trust and faith. Simon went even though he didn't have the money, only to learn that he had an unexpected benefactor. This is the awesome and delightful way of the Divine!

When we commit to creating a vision then show up and do the work, the Divine will bring people and resources to support and make manifest that which serves us, others, and is in Divine order. Know that some "tweaking" will occur because the Divine knows your purpose, and He has a bigger vision for you than you could ever have for yourself. So *be* open and trust in You and the Divine as he organizes the details. Be bold! Then watch the magic unfold!

57

You Love Me

You love me deeply,
Deliciously,
Stirringly,
To the heights of who I Am,
To the depths of my Soul.
I always had wings,
But didn't seem to know.
You gave me air,
Lifting me to joy.
You showed me myself.
You showed me the way.
Thank you for You,
Thank you for who,
You have been and more.
So much,
So soulful,
So, so, so...
I need say nothing more.

Journey's End... Until We Begin Again

58

Surrender to Trust

We come into the world bright-eyed, innocent, and expecting the good and true of Life. It is our nature to trust. Over time, the world reveals itself to us—eroding away our innocence and trust through disappointment, abandonment, or trauma. We learn to trust some people but not others, and even those who are very reliable falter at some point. This process causes us to forget that we are expressions of the Divine, our Oneness with Him, and our purpose here. We forget that we can trust the One for everything.

Do you remember the many times you've heard a soft whisper guiding you or a thought that wasn't your own directing you? Do you remember that you always had a problem when you didn't honor what you were told? This was your Spirit speaking to you. This was the Divine speaking to you! When you think about it, His record is impeccable and spans years or decades—your whole life, in fact. No one else has this kind of track record! Neither would you require this of anyone before you trusted them. An unwillingness to trust the Divine is a barrier to aligning with Him and your Divine Self.

Failure to trust the Divine is akin to giving up a lookout, who sits high upon a hill and sees the lay of the land. He sees the best routes, watering holes, food, secure shelter, and the best way for you to prosper. He also sees the pitfalls, obstacles, and those who would stand against you; and He will provide a way out or sustain you as you make your way through. An unwillingness to trust the One means giving all of that away and fending for yourself. Many of us do just that! Many of us wander through Life feeling as though we've been forsaken in the wilderness when it is we who have forsaken His guidance and protection in our desire to do it ourselves.

When our human self stops trying to figure things out and we trust in our Oneness, our Spirit emerges to guide and inform us. The Divine and the Universe are abundant, infinite, and capable of providing anything asked for from a place of love, integrity, and service. No need has to go unmet because the Divine is everything, and we are One with the Divine. We are all everything.

Know that you are always creating. This is guided by doing or Being. When Spirit or Being guides this process, you can have the intention to create one thing but are in full acceptance when something else shows up because you trust that this is what was needed to serve you and others at this time. You aren't trapped in the resistance of wanting people and situations to be something other than they are because your Spirit knows the perfection of everything. This includes the perfection of people, events, and the timing of the interaction between the two. You trust that everything is in Divine order and serves the transformation of everyone. Your Spirit knows who and what you require for this to occur during your stay on the planet. It also knows when based upon your preparedness, and it is all done in love.

This includes the storms of life. It may not seem or feel like it, but rest assured, it is all happening in order to bring you back to You, your Divine Self. There is a saying that God doesn't close a door without opening a window. In the past, you might have said, "I don't want that! That's not what I asked for! I want a red door with raised panels and brass hardware—not a window!" Now, you trust the perfection of everything, which allows you to choose again based on what is before you. You create in this way, moment after moment, moving through the window presented to you when the door closes.

Your actions are guided by answers to the following questions: "What is required of me?" and "What must I do for this situation?" Having done this, you will notice a peace that settles upon you. You no longer have to figure things out on your own because you are connected to and guided by That which knows all. So It knows what will serve You and others at all times. You trust that what is before you and what you must do in response to it will work out because it is all designed to pull you forward. You trust this even when it would appear otherwise, and you continue to walk the path set before you. You trust it because this knowing was given to your Spirit by the One Universal Wisdom. This absolute knowing gives you ease and tranquility.

Trusting in this way allows you to surrender. The two are intimately intertwined. Surrender is often met with great resistance because we believe we are surrendering to something unknown, unfamiliar, and unpredictable—something outside our self. We do not recognize that we are surrendering to our Self, our Divine Self, when we surrender to the Divine. Surrender may come as an act of capitulation when all other options have been exhausted, when we are exhausted. First, we surrender our beliefs then our way of doing things. This means giving up all the beliefs we ever had about ourselves then giving up our beliefs about others and events. These beliefs led us to take certain actions, many of which haven't worked out well. This was decided based upon intellect. This is doing. This results in frustration, confusion, and pain for ourselves and others. We are compelled to cry out, "Help me!" The Divine always hears you and always answers.

Surrender may also be the result of awakening to your Divinity and the One Universal Source. The recognition of and trust in your Oneness enable you to bow your head and surrender. This is your human self, also known as the ego, bowing to the Divine and the Divinity within you. Now, you can lift your head and arms in celebration and exultation of your unity with the Divine. Asking, "How may I serve?" takes on an entirely new dimension. You are asking, "How may I serve the Universe, Humanity and the greater good?" by aligning yourself with the will and knowledge of the

Divine that is all knowing and Universal Consciousness. You gain absolute certainty from this unity knowing that You honor and serve the Divine order of everything. You were the slave of your ego. You are now the servant of the Divine energy of the Universe and Humanity. This serves You and your purpose for being here at this time. You serve with grace knowing that You serve the One, regardless of who others are and the disguises they have donned. You have trusted in and surrendered to Your Divine Self, to the One, and to the One within us all. You have been released from your human shackles and are free to live infinitely!

This is an invitation to trust in and surrender to the One and Your Oneness with everything. Trust in the One because "I knew you before I formed you in your mother's womb.[15] Trust in the One because He is always with you and You with Him. Trust in the One because You and He are One and everything is available through the One. He can be your everything, and we are everything with Him.

59

Acceptance

*"You see that chair. It has certain functions. You can
sit on it, stand on it, or put things on it; it provides
some level of support. But if you try to get it to ride
you to work, you're going to have some problems."*

~ Balin A. Durr, M.D.

Something happens in each and every moment. There's never a moment when nothing is happening. Even when we are sleeping, our bodies are hard at work. The sun is rising on the other side of the world, and stars are being born. Once it occurs, whatever it is, it already exists and cannot be changed, regardless of our wishes, desires, or regrets. When we resist what is, our energy, resources, and vision are tied up in the resistance.

Resistance is evoked when something is judged as negative or undesirable. Judgment and compartmentalization of people and events occur when we fail to recognize that everything is One with the Divine. Resistance becomes a veil between us and

Spirit, separating us from our Divine Self. This barrier causes us to operate out of intellect and habit. Our focus shifts to contents of the world and away from Being. The world becomes our center. We get caught up, giving attention and energy to what's going on in the world. We believe we are the events and the events are important. Our sense of Self is lost in the process.

There is the moment, and there are the events that occur in the moment. We are just as incapable of bypassing this moment as we are moving directly from kindergarten to 9th grade, having bypassed 2nd through 8th grade. You cannot reach your desired future by leaping over today or this moment. Your grand future is built one moment at a time just as the Great Wall of China and the Pyramids at Giza were built—one brick at a time. Each one is just as important as the next because there can be no grand tomorrow built on a shaky, substandard today. Many of us have created lives with holes and gaps because we didn't want to sit with, be with, or acknowledge Life as it was at that time. This failure to acknowledge what was and learn from it left some feeling hollow and others with a Life in all out collapse due to deficient, shoddy workmanship. We weren't willing to do the work, and the weight of Life collapsed upon our heads. We created more chaos and drama by resisting Life.

Living in the moment means you are in acceptance of everything as it is. No alterations, variations, or adaptations. Acceptance neither sanctions nor validates an occurrence. *Acceptance is acknowledgment only.* You aren't stuck with things as they are. On the contrary, you make a choice based upon what is instead of how you wish it to be. You understand that this moment can't be changed, and your response is for a future outcome.

For example, you formulate a response when an injustice occurs, and you're not stuck in, "This shouldn't have happened!" or "This is awful!" Instead, you ask, "What does this moment require of me?" or "How may I serve?" You are free to create something phenomenal from an infinite number of possibilities, having moved to a place of accepting people and situations as they are. You are in alignment with what is, and your response serves the Divine order of everything.

Acceptance is a powerful way of Being in the world! Acceptance of what happens in Life is alignment with the Divine Universal Source that is Life. This is communion with the Divine—spiritual union with the Divine, with Life itself. This is Oneness. This is Being with the One. This is Being the One. You are no longer bound, no longer tied to that which held you for so long. You choose to create anew from this inspired space. Oneness guides your responses and serves the sacredness of all Life. The Universe opens up in abundance.

60

Free to Be

"You can lead a horse to water, but you can't make him swim."

~ Christopher Albert,
six years of age

Attachment to things in the world causes us to believe we are of the world. Attachment strengthens our ego, our sense of our self as human, and separates us from our perception as an eternal Soul having a human experience. We believe we are our body, clothes, occupation, residence, relationships, political connections, and accomplishments or perceived failures. This is like believing you are the debris in the river that is being swept away by the current instead of recognizing that You are the Soul that is the Observer sitting on the river bank watching the debris go by. Or think of it this way. You're like an eagle that believes it's a turkey when your identity and happiness are attached to things! You see yourself as grounded, awkward, limited, and possibly dinner instead of a soaring, majestic, limitless Spirit! The things of your life are tools to serve you during your time on the planet. They are NOT you and aren't meant to define you. You are to possess them. They are NOT to possess you.

The flow of Divine Consciousness through us is disturbed and inevitably blocked when we introduce an intention and are attached to the outcome. This energy flow is dammed by our unwillingness to let go. In its most destructive form, attachment becomes a grasping, wrenching force that causes swirling stagnation, decay, and suffering. We cling to what could have been and miss out on limitless possibilities. This magical Universe will surprise and amaze you if you allow it to unfold based upon Its wisdom instead of imposing restrictive limitations due to your driving fears.

When you introduce an intention to create something, remain open to what shows up. The flow continues undisturbed because your response is creative, spontaneous, and serves the needs of that which is before you. You flow with it and continue to create with what is available instead of creating suffering because what you hoped for didn't manifest. You trust that Universal Wisdom presents to you that which serves your transformation and your highest interest. It's what's supposed to occur and the perfect time for it to do so. That includes the opportunity to reject potentially harmful situations that don't reflect your highest Self. Remember, in order to know who You are, You have to know who you are not.

Enjoy the journey! Having a myopic focus on the destination prevents us from enjoying the sights along the way. We miss out on the joy, beauty, opportunity, and splendor of the moment because we weren't fully present or engaged. Having an intention or goal is important, but you must be nimble, alert, and willing to adapt when the unexpected appears before you. Set an intention and know there are many paths to get you there. Some have spectacular scenery, but all have pearls that you'll need for the rest of your journey. When you reach the end of this lifetime and look back over your life, what will matter is the love shared with others, the unexpected joys and surprises, and the difference you made in the lives of others.

Imagine that you've decided to take a walk along a forest trail. You could make it a brisk walk, but you decide to take a leisurely stroll upon entering the forest. You see the explosion of color from the beautiful flowers and inhale their intoxicating scent. The sun caresses your skin, and you lift your face heavenward to bask in its warm rays. Some of the animals scamper along the forest floor while others jump from branch to branch. Still, others can be seen soaring high above in the sky. The trees stand like towering sentries, providing shade along the way. As you pause, you hear the gurgling water of a distant stream. You take a deep breath and exhale. Your eyes are closed, your head is tilted back, and your arms are spread wide open. You feel Life all about you. You hear birds twitter, squirrels chatter, and trees seeming to speak to each other as their leaves rustle in the wind.

You continue along the path, pausing many times to take in the discoveries and some surprises. One occurred as you emerged from the canopy of trees onto a platform to suddenly find yourself peering at majestic snow-capped mountains that seem to touch the sky and a stunning valley below covered in lush green grass with a river winding through it. It takes your breath away! All you can do is stand there and take it in, marveling at the magnificence before you. Eventually, you return to the trail and continue to enjoy the natural beauty all around you. You come to the end—having completed a delightful journey! You have smiled many times, but this is a wistful smile because you wish it would go on; however, you know that you will do this again.

This is Life. Creation made manifest with surprising discoveries along the way. It was delightful, magnificent, joyful, and serene! This can be your Life if you remain open to the manifestations of your intentions. Initially, you planned to take a brisk walk, but you were spontaneous, flexible, and eager to take advantage of the opportunities that presented themselves. You slowed down and enjoyed the beauty of nature instead of insisting that you had to follow through with your initial plan. You didn't force yourself to take the brisk walk but flowed with nature instead. You remained open to what the Divine had in store for you instead of tied to what you wanted for yourself. This allowed Life to reveal itself in spectacular and unexpected ways!

I still remember the first time I heard the opening quote. It was delightful, and I laughed a lot! It quickly became a favorite. I was struck by the fact that this baby, this little One, knew what many have forgotten on the journey. Remain unattached and delight in the magic of the Universe! Detachment allows You to define yourself in a way that surpasses something that is temporary and limited in capacity. You are free to *be* a Soul that is neither subject to the winds of time nor anything in the physical universe. You are open to the manifestations of your intentions because Divine Universal Consciousness flows through you, and the Universe is abundant! You are a Soul that is eternal, forever, and boundless. You are limitless!

61

Communion

Every day, every bird seen flying in the sky, every heartbeat, every glimpse of the Soul of another is a chance to commune with God—to connect with our Source, to connect with our Self. It is the One to the One. It is the One with the One. Everything and everyone is sacred because everything is an expression of the Divine. Every encounter allows us to experience our Self in every moment. You might call it something else, a blessing perhaps, but the experience and they are sacred in that they share, endure, and yes, suffer so that we might grow into and experience our Divinity here on the planet. They are deserving of our deep gratitude and regard for the gift of communion—spiritual union. It has all been for this end.

Every occurrence in every moment can *be* a spiritual practice. It's an opportunity to practice Being connected all of the time, to know Eternity all of the time. Bring this knowing to every waking moment, and experience the joy and magic that is Life, that is *your* sacred Life, and is the ONE. Welcome Home! Home always awaits You. You return back to the One who loved You first, back to the One who loved You always. You are called to love as He does and to give it away. You can do this because You always have it within You. You always have Him, and therefore, everything within You. You have my deep gratitude for taking this journey with Me. May You be a blessing to all You encounter and to all You serve. May the Divinity in all things rise up to meet You, and may you live in the fullness granted to You by the Divine.

Namasté,
Balin A. Durr, M.D.

Notes

1. Washington, James Jr, Deloris Tarzan Ament Interview with James Washington Jr., November 12, 1999.
2. Shakespeare, William, *Romeo and Juliet*, Act II, Scene II, The Oxford Shakespeare, 1914.
3. de Chardin, Pierre Teilhard, *The Phenomenon of Man*, (New York: Harper & Brothers, 1959).
4. Exod. 3:14 KJV
5. Dyer, Wayne, "Wayne Dyer in Maui," *Super Soul Sunday*, season 3, episode 7, aired July 15, 2012.
6. Beckwith, Dr. Michael Bernard, "The Answer Is You," *PBS program*, aired September 23, 2009.
7. *Tyler Perry's Madea's Family Reunion,* film, directed by Tyler Perry (Atlanta, GA: Tyler Perry Productions. February 24, 2006), DVD.
8. Luke 23:34 KJV
9. Jakes, Rev T.D., "Live with Purpose," *Oprah's Lifeclass*, aired April 9, 2012.
10. *The Great Debaters*, film, directed by Denzel Washington (Santa Monica, CA: The Weinstein Company/Genius Products. May 13, 2008), DVD.

11. Winfrey, Oprah, "Finding Inner Peace and Happiness with Michael Singer," *Super Soul Sunday*, aired October 28, 2012.

12. Walsch, Neale Donald, *Communion with God*, (New York: Berkley Books, 2002).

13. Vanzant, Iyanla,"The Power of Forgiveness," *Oprah's Lifeclass: The Tour*, aired April 16, 2012.

14. Handler, Chelsea, "Chelsea Handler," *Oprah's Next Chapter*, aired March 10, 2013.

15. Jeremiah 1:5 NLT

Stay Connected!

Dr. Durr is an author, poet, and psychiatrist for children, adolescents, and adults. She conceptualized the term *Sacred Arts* as a holistic melding of medical and spiritual healing via artistic expression. *Heaven Abounds in You: The Journey to Joy* is her first endeavor in this realm. May this enlighten and inspire you on your journey.

Other titles will follow soon.

Connect with or follow Dr. Durr at:
www.BalinADurrMD.com
Facebook: /BalinADurrMD
Twitter: @BalinADurrMD
LinkedIn: BalinADurrMD

CPSIA information can be obtained at www.ICGtesting.com
Printed in the USA
LVOW06s0112081015

457425LV00001B/161/P